Hehring

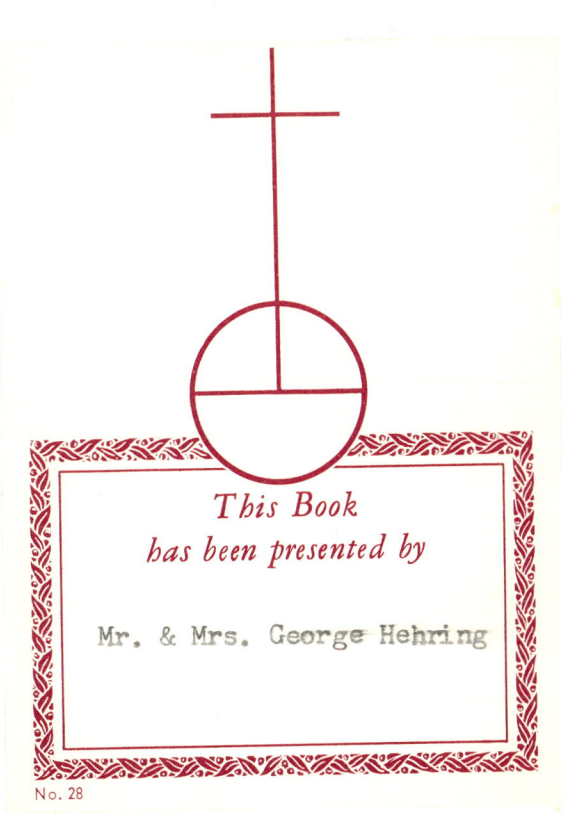

*This Book
has been presented by*

Mr. & Mrs. George Hehring

No. 28

Don't Put On Your Slippers Yet

Don't Put On Your Slippers Yet

Colena M. Anderson

FIRST LUTHERAN CHURCH OF GRAY MANOR
LIBRARY
212 Oakwood Road
Baltimore, Md. 21222

zondervan publishing house OF THE ZONDERVAN CORPORATION
GRAND RAPIDS, MICHIGAN 49506

Don't Put on Your Slippers Yet
© 1971 by Zondervan Publishing House
Grand Rapids, Michigan

Fourth printing 1974
Sixth printing (Large Type Edition) 1978

Unless otherwise specified all quotations from the Bible in this volume are from the Revised Standard Version of the Bible, © 1946 and 1952 by the Division of Christian Education of the National Council of Churches in the United States of America. Used by special permission.

Library of Congress Catalog Card Number 72-171196
ISBN 0-310-20027-X

All rights reserved. No portion of this book may be used in any form without the written permission of the publisher, with the exception of brief excerpts in magazine reviews, etc.

Printed in the United States of America

To my mother,
FRANCES MICHAEL,
*who in all of her thirty years
past sixty-five
gave no thought to retirement*

CONTENTS

1. "Good-by, Have Fun" 9
2. Hankering for the Fleshpots 19
3. Approaching the Growing Edge 33
4. A Cloud of Witnesses 45
5. Bring Me the Book 59
6. Bridging the Gap 73
7. When Death Steps In 85
8. The Fifth Blessing 97

Appendix 109

"GOOD-BY, HAVE FUN"

1 "GOOD-BY, HAVE FUN"

The day had finally come, long anticipated and now most welcome. With his wife Martha beside him at the flower-bedecked banquet table, Bill Vance sat blinking his eyes while his fellow workers from the print shop sang, "For he's a jolly good fellow." In front of him, besides a "Congratulations and Best Wishes for Your Retirement" card and a gold, no-wind, perpetual calendar wrist watch, there was a package marked "To be opened tomorrow morning."

How often during the past year the projected image of this event had come to his mind! Twelve months ago he had begun a secret countdown of months: 12, 11, 10 . . . 4, 3, 2 — and then had switched to days: 30, 29, 28 . . . 4, 3, 2, 1 — it was here, the Day of Retirement.

No more punching the time clock. No more taking orders from anyone. No more meeting deadlines. No more having to hear that young, green whippersnapper of an office boy calling him "Grandpa." Free! For the first time in his life he was his own man. Tonight he could say,

> "Farewell, thou busy world, and may
> We never meet again." [1]

Earlier in the day, across town, Donna Swanson put down her sixth grade roll book, choked up as her pupils filed by: "Good-by, teacher. Have a good summer." "S'long, Mrs. Swanson. Have fun." — and found her own well-rehearsed farewell speech condensed into an unsteady "Good-by. God bless you all."

When the last youngster had gone, she tucked the small presents that some of the class had shyly placed on her desk into her carry-all, empty now of corrected homework, half-guessed answers to tests, and books for that bonus time of sharing gifts of mind and spirit.

Last week the faculty had had a farewell dinner for her. Tonight she ate alone. At the window overlooking her small garden, she sat down to a bowl of cereal and milk. She had no appetite for more. In the western sky the rose and gold of the June sunset gave way to the lavender of twilight.

Twenty-one years ago she had watched a sunset much like this one. Carl was at her side then. They had had a quiet twenty-fifth wedding anniversary dinner at home by themselves. The children were away: Alice, their oldest, was married, living across the continent; John was at college; Laura, their youngest, was in the nearby hospital undergoing a battery of tests.

---

[1] Charles Cotton, "The Retirement," from *Songs of Nature*, John Burroughs, ed., Doubleday, Page and Co., 1912, p. 1.

Slipping his arm around Donna and drawing her close, Carl had said, "Beautiful sunset. I think the portal of heaven will be like that."

In the morning when she awoke, he had already entered the portal.

"Coronary," the doctor pronounced. Then, laying his hand on her shoulder, "You're strong. You have faith. You'll make it."

Would she make it? John still in college. Laura — what would the tests show? Alone now. How could she make it without Carl?

Billow after billow of grief had washed over her, and she felt herself drowning in the depths. Then, as though physical arms lifted her, she felt herself sustained, and for a moment between each deluge she found herself praying, "God, help me. God, help me make it."

Now, twenty-one years later, she was reviewing the road from then to now. John had wanted to stop college, but she had urged him to continue. "Dad would want you to. Remember how happy he was when you told us you wanted to be a doctor? What you'll be able to earn yourself plus part of dad's insurance will see you through." And so it had. Now John was overseas helping to mend the bodies of the victims of war.

And there was Laura. Dear, dear girl, how patient and cheerful she had been during those ten long years of being in and out of hospitals. And then they had to lay her frail body to rest close to Carl's.

Carl.... The remainder of his insurance had eased the financial strain of those ten years and that first year when Donna had to return to college to get her teaching certificate. What would they have done without that $20,000, long since gone?

"You'll make it." The doctor's words of twenty-one years ago echoed in Donna's mind. At that time she had asked, "Will I? How can I without Carl?"

Now she was asking, "Did I make it? Truly make it?" If twenty years of teaching, the first half of which had been weighted with the aching concern over Laura, could be called "making it," then perhaps she had — at least outwardly. But inwardly, does a widow ever really conquer the sense of being half a person?

"Slipping into the slough of self-pity. This will never do, Donna." Talking to herself again! Last week in conversation with a friend who was teaching in the Psychology Department of the nearby college, when Donna had jokingly asked, "What do you psychologists say about a person who talks to herself?" the friend had replied, "I don't want to tell you here, but I'll give you a book. You can read for yourself." Was she joking or was she serious? No matter. There were times when a person had to talk to herself.

But she didn't have to wallow in self-pity. She could always get up and do something. Automatically she reached for pad and pencil, familiar objects that had so often steadied her.

The red pencil now in her hand was geared to figuring. Going to her desk and turning on the shaded lamp, she set down a simple problem in old-fashioned addition.

Social Security	$2160
Retirement Fund	1200
Bank Interest	150
Dividends	800

Compared with her salary of last year, $10,620.00, $4,310.00 was quite a drop. But at that, it was more than she had been paid when she first started to teach. That first year her wage slip for income tax was $3,500.00. It had taken long years to come to the five digit salary. No wonder then that with trips East to see Alice, the several needed paintings of the house, the new furnace, the roofing of house and garage, the rewiring of the house after the attic fire, and dozens of other extra necessities, she had not been able to invest more than $10,000 in mutual funds and to date had only $3,300.00 in the bank.

She checked the sum, then stared at the first two figures. What, she wondered, what if something should happen to the other figures? Remembering the financial debacle of 1929 and the recent stock market slump, she found the "what if" pregnant with apprehension.

Fortunately, she recalled the article she had seen last week in the dentist's office. It was in a back issue of *Modern Maturity,* titled "Are You Eating Properly?" At the bottom of the page in large print was the statement:

> The body functions more slowly with the years; fewer calories are needed to keep it running.[2]

Fewer calories meant less food. Less food meant lower grocery bills. In that case, if she ended with only social security and retirement fund, she wouldn't starve, would she?

Somewhat reassured, she chided herself for selfish worrying when she knew that thousands of retired and non-retired persons in the country and in the world

[2] Vol. 11, No. 4, p. 67.

had families to feed on less than she would be receiving. With that thought she went to bed, remembering not to turn on the alarm. Tomorrow she could sleep as long as she wished.

Before sleep came, she found herself longing for a hand on her shoulder and a voice saying, "You're strong. You'll make it." In the absence of both, she prayed again, "God, help me. Help me make it through my retirement."

Martha and Bill rode home together through the late evening. Halfway there, Bill said, "Nice feeling to know we won't suddenly be plunged to a lower bracket of income. I've just been figuring in my head. Returns from that annuity we began the first year we were married, plus social security, plus interest on the first mortgages that we hold, plus dividends and capital gains on those lucky investments will bring our yearly income close to what I was getting last year in wages. Not bad, is it? Thanks to you, Martha. You've been a good, frugal wife."

"Don't forget, Bill, we've had no expenses for — for children. It wouldn't have been so easy to save if——"

Bill drew her close. "Oh, you'd have managed." His tone was tender, for he knew and shared her loneliness.

When they turned into their own yard, Bill broke the silence. "Tomorrow," he gloated, "I don't have to set the alarm. Tomorrow I'll sleep as long as I want to. And, Martha, don't you wake me."

The next day, though, he woke before dawn, earlier than he had ever wakened — even with an alarm. After several ineffectual attempts to woo back sleep, he threw off the covers and got up.

In the process of dressing, as he was about to put

on his shoes, he remembered the package marked "To be opened tomorrow." When he opened it, he found a pair of new, soft-soled slippers and a note: "A gift for your Golden Years, symbol of the ease that is now your due. Hope you'll wear these for a long, long time. Good-by. Have fun."

Bill smiled, shoved his old shoes under a closet shelf, and put on the new slippers. Such soft, comfortable slippers!

Then he remembered his plan for the day. He was going to spade up another vegetable plot in the backyard and enlarge the border for flowers. He certainly could not wear these new slippers for that.

Bending over, he took them off, admired them for a moment, and then went to the closet and exchanged them for his old, worn shoes.

Seeing that Martha was still asleep, he tiptoed from the bedroom. In the kitchen, setting the coffee to perk, he whistled, "Oh, what a beautiful morning. Oh, what a beautiful day."

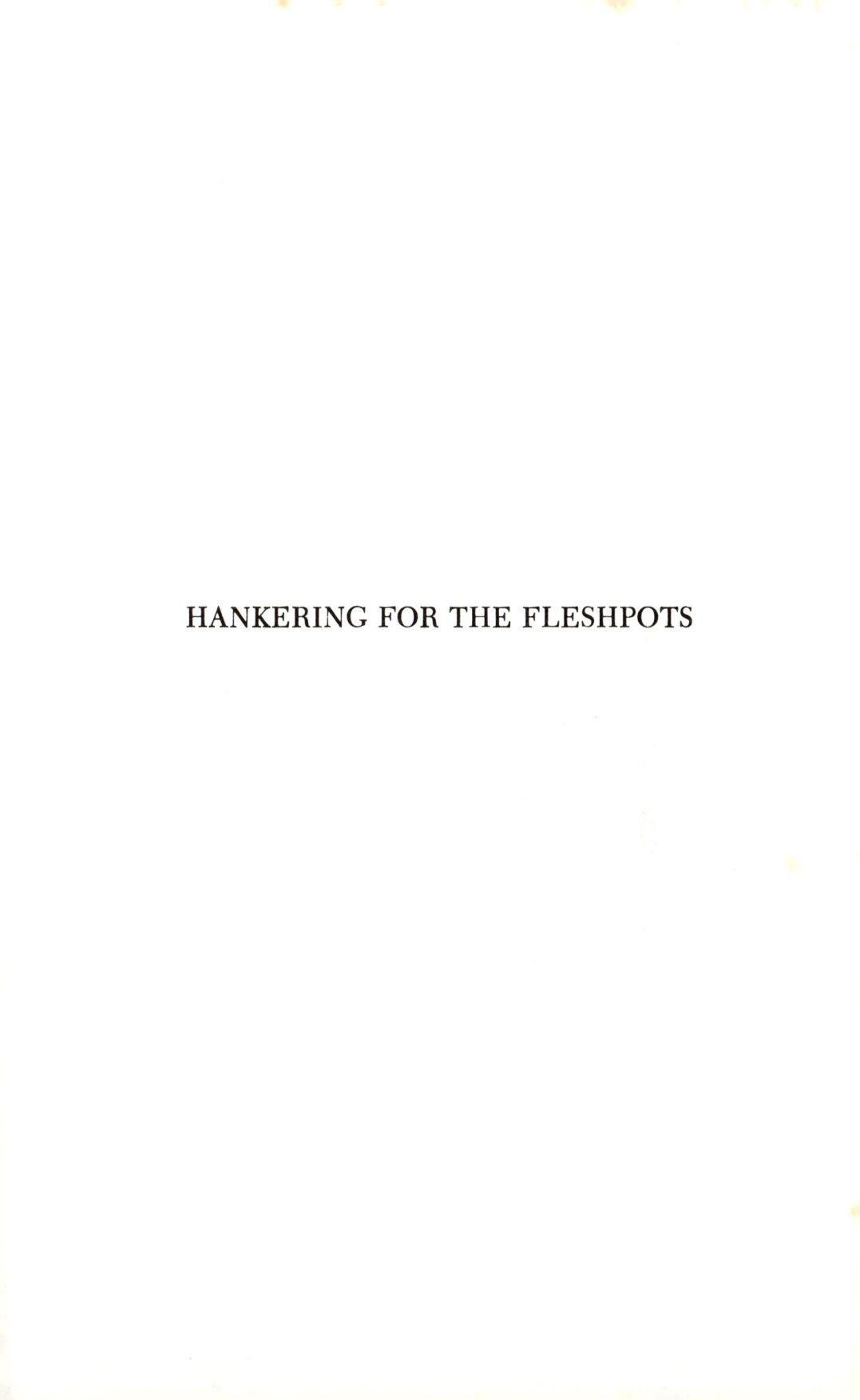

HANKERING FOR THE FLESHPOTS

2 HANKERING FOR THE FLESHPOTS

Three months had passed since Bill's retirement banquet. Through the remainder of June and all through July and August his initial exuberance had stayed with him. He and Martha had taken several weekend trips out of state, and frequently during the week they would spend a day at the beach, less than a hundred miles from home, or go to one of the state parks or visit friends.

Then, too, he enjoyed working in his backyard garden. He had never had so much time to give to it. Now daily he shared tomatoes, carrots, summer squash, and cucumbers with neighbors, and as he went from house to house he took note that nowhere were Peace roses as large as his.

"Did you ever see such a rose as this, Martha?"

"No, I never did. Your thumb has certainly grown

green this summer. Nice that you have that garden to putter in. Keeps you happy outdoors. I'm real thankful for that."

Now what did she mean? Not thankful for all the fresh vegetables? Just thankful that he was happy outdoors? What was behind her queer smile?

Not until mid-September did the answer come. It was a rainy Saturday, too wet to work in the garden, so he settled himself comfortably in the living room to watch TV. Engrossed in a rerun of one of the early football games, he was oblivious to Martha's entrance with the vacuum until the picture began to flicker. As she came close to his chair, he turned to say, "Please shut that off, Martha." But seeing how intent she was with her cleaning, he kept silent and accommodatingly moved his chair. Three times he moved it.

Then at the most exciting play of the game, Martha snapped off the vacuum and, arms akimbo, said in a voice close to a shout, "Bill, I wish you'd leave me alone here to finish this room. Go out to the garden or take a walk. Go see how Jeff is getting along."

Persona non grata in his own house! He never thought that would happen to him. "Go see Jeff!" Jeff — the talking parrot at the print shop!

In all his working days Martha had never treated him like this. But then, he had to admit, he'd never been home often on Saturdays. And — a brand-new thought struck him — her regular work continued day after day.

He had heard and read jokes and seen cartoons about the husband-wife relationship after a husband's retirement and had chuckled over them, but now —

"Go see Jeff." He couldn't get rid of the directive.

It kept echoing in his mind as, shoulders hunched under his raincoat, he walked down to the print shop. He was going, not to see Jeff, but to accept the offer of his old boss: "Anytime you feel like coming down for part-time work, Bill, we surely could use you."

He didn't need the money, but that brand-new thought about Martha had put the idea into his head that if he went back to work a few hours each day, especially on Saturdays, she'd have the house to herself. It was a purely unselfish motive.

At the shop the smell of ink and the hum of the presses sent a wave of nostalgia through him. Here was meaningful action. Here a man could feel he was contributing to the work of the world. How could he have been so thoroughly glad to leave the place? By the time he reached the head office, the idea stemming from his brand-new thought about Martha's non-retirement was no longer purely unselfish. He wanted to come back for his own sake.

"Part-time work, Mr. Vance?" the new boss was saying. "Sorry. We're full up. Now if you had come a month ago——"

But a month ago Bill was still riding high on the freedom of his retirement.

On his way out, the old friends called above the hum: "Hi, lucky you." "You're looking great." "Life of Riley agrees with you." But that was all; there was no time for chitchat.

As he opened the door to leave, Jeff, the parrot, called, "S'long, pal. Where yuh goin'?" Like a refrain on a warped record, the words followed him down to the street: "Where yuh goin'? Where yuh goin'?"

Where? Well, he was going to find out whether

other retirees ever had a longing to go back to their old jobs, and if so, what they did about it.

By the time he reached the city park at the library, the rain had stopped and, characteristic of Oregon weather, the sun came out full-face and warm. In the park seventy-year-old Sam Perkins was laying newspapers on a damp bench.

"Put one down for me too, Sam," Bill called. "I want to ask you a question."

"Ask away." Sam settled himself gingerly. "Can't stay too long."

"I'll make it short. What I'd like to know is how you felt after you retired from that gas station you'd operated for so long."

"Well now," Sam drawled, "soon after I gave up the station, I just found my feet naturally going back. Bothered my successor so much he finally sent me over to the new station two miles down the highway on the other side. Just to get rid of me, I know, but he did me a good turn. Yes sir-ee, he did. That new young fellow gave me part-time work. And you know what?" Sam chuckled. "Lots of my old customers came over there. Guess I did him a good turn too."

That night after deacon's meeting at the church, Bill buttonholed the ex-president of the local college. "Two years now since you retired, Prexy." (The whole town still called him "Prexy.") "Are you willing to tell me how you felt during those first few months? Did you ever long to go back?"

"Months? For a whole year. I deliberately stayed off the campus. Not easy; one doesn't break the habit of more than a quarter of century without withdrawal pains."

Hankering for the Fleshpots

Prexy put his hand on Bill's shoulder. "You know what we retirees need? A kind of R.A. — Retirees Anonymous, like the A.A. Comes a time, sooner or later, when each of us needs a sympathetic, listening ear." Reaching into his pocket, he pulled out a card. "Here's my phone number. I'll be glad to listen to you anytime."

On his way home, Bill studied the card. In the lower left-hand corner he read, "U.S. representative of Overseas Investors."

"*Et, tu*, Prexy," Bill said to himself.

By September Donna Swanson was having her bout with retirement malaise. The summer hadn't been too bad. She had always used these vacation months to catch up on her reading. On the day of her retirement a dozen books waited for her to turn their pages. But by the end of August she had turned all of them, having read so fast that the plots had become jumbled and thoroughly integrated. When she went to her oculist, she was shocked at the price of new glasses. How could the cost have increased so much since the last time she had needed a new prescription?

Months ago she had dreamed of long, unhurried shopping sprees. She soon discovered, however, that the pleasure of shopping is in direct ratio to the bulge of one's purse, and these days her purse was embarrassingly slim.

Also she had promised herself to use part of her leisure hours to clean the house. There never had been enough time while she was teaching. Now by mid-September every window was sparkling, every closet was in order, all the linens were carefully ironed, and all the silver was polished.

For a week she had been watching the children as they passed her house to and from school. Knowing she was no longer a part of the parade plunged her into depression. Someone had said, "The only way to combat the feeling is to meet it head-on. Go back to the old haunts and see——" See what?

"You tell by trying" was the motto on the board in the psychology seminar where she had met Carl. In those faraway college days the motto had been good for many a jocular testing. Now she was serious. Walking along the familiar route, she felt excitement quicken within her the way it used to do when she had some special project planned. Then suddenly the feeling faded, and she knew it had been but the echo of a past happiness.

Once inside the door of the school, out of long habit, she automatically went to the faculty mailboxes. Some summer mail might be there. She began dialing the number, 5, 9——

"Uh, uh!" Someone close put out a detaining hand.

"Oh, I beg your pardon. For a moment, I forgot."

"Well, now you know." The stranger laughed, dialed, turned the knob, opened the box, and took out a handful of her own personal mail.

Classes were forming. The old friends were busy. They had time only to nod, to wave a hand, to call, "Hi. How are you?" One voice rose above the others, "What are you doing here? I thought you were retired."

So I am, Donna said to herself as she turned homeward. And what was I doing there anyway?

Hankering for the fleshpots! The words came full-blown as though someone outside herself were answering her question, speaking truth in all its painful simplicity.

Back home she hunted up the passage about the fleshpots of Egypt.

> They set out from Elim, and all the congregation of the people of Israel came to the wilderness of Sin, which is between Elim and Sinai, on the fifteenth day of the second month after they had departed from the land of Egypt. And the whole congregation of the people of Israel murmured against Moses and Aaron in the wilderness, and said to them, "Would that we had died by the hand of the Lord in the land of Egypt, when we sat by the fleshpots and ate bread to the full; for you have brought us out into this wilderness to kill the whole assembly with hunger" (Exodus 16:1-3).

After closing the Bible, she laid it gently on the table. How close she was to those Israelite murmurers! They were in a physical wilderness; she was in a psychological one. They were hungry for the fleshpots of kids' meat and lentils and garlic, for the rich gravies they scooped up in little pancake loaves bent like spoons. She was hungry for classes of children, for the bubbling stews of exciting projects, hungry even for the meetings she used to think were bores: faculty, committees, PTA, NEA. Why should she have thought them so boring? They and her classes had kept her constantly on the growing edge of life.

Through the rest of the morning nervous tension mounted. By early afternoon she felt she must get out of the house. Where should she go? "Where the wind blows us," Carl used to say, meaning "Where the Lord leads us."

That day the wind blew her to Joan Williams, a college classmate living some twenty miles away. It was a full year now since Joan had left her position as private secretary to a lawyer in Portland, Oregon. Her friends knew her as the one who had an uncanny ability for giving timely help. Invite her to a dinner party and find out, too late to go to the store, that you'd forgotten to get lemons for the iced tea, and when Joan arrived she'd have one of the lemon-shaped plastic squeeze bottles full of lemon juice. Or come vacation time when your six-year-old grandson was with you for a week and you'd forgotten your promise to spend the afternoon at the Workshop for the Blind, there Joan would be on the phone, lilting in her happy voice, "I'm taking some neighbor kids to the swimming pool. Wouldn't Johnny like to come along?"

When you asked her, "How did you know I needed this juice?" or "How did you know I was wondering what to do with Johnny this afternoon?" Joan would only raise her eyebrows and shrug her shoulders.

This afternoon Donna found her sorting out old magazines. "They gather so quickly," Joan said. "I try to pass them on, but so many people say now, 'I'd rather watch TV.' Maybe, though, you——" Joan began rummaging through the copies. "Yes, here they are, these two copies have articles that I thought would interest you." She opened one to an article titled "Retirement Is a State of Mind," and another to a column headed "Teachers Take to New Jobs."

"Needn't read them now, Donna. Take them home. You may find some other helps."

Donna took the magazines, saw the names — *NRTA Journal,* and knew they were published by the National Retired Teachers Association. Last June she had been invited to join that association but had declined, saying, "I'm not a joiner. Associations and conventions bore me." Now as she gave the articles a cursory glance, she knew that they would help her in her present state of restlessness and hankering. "Helps," she echoed Joan's word. "How did you know I need encouragement today?"

Joan shrugged her shoulders. "Don't we all during the first months of retirement? I'll never forget my spell of home — no, better call it office-sickness. I had such a longing for that office that I did the foolish thing of going back two weeks after I'd left. My employer was out. The new young secretary greeted me quite formally, took my name, and said, 'I shall inform Mr. Davis that you called.'

"In those two weeks she had shifted the desk, rearranged the books, and exchanged the seascapes that Mr. Davis liked for some frightful 'I-dare-you-to-know-what-I-am' abstract paintings.

"I tell you, Donna, once you're out, there's no going back. You've got to find a new stamping ground for yourself. And if you want to do more than just go stamping around, you have to do what that other article says. Now which one was that?"

Joan reached for one of the copies that Donna was holding and began running her finger down the Table of Contents. "Ah, yes, here it is. 'Put Your Talent to Work.' The writer certainly hits the nail on the head: 'Tensions [she must mean "Pensions"] and social security do not buy the life we were used to living before retirement.' Then she goes on to report the new occupations that persons whom she interviewed told her about. Two women are giving professional shopping reports. Partners now, they have five-figure incomes. And here are suggestions for making money using your car and your house. Make money and give needed services at the same time. And this one should interest you — use your speaking talents to give talks. Dozens of suggestions." [1]

"How have you put your talent to work?" Donna asked after Joan handed back the magazine.

"Not exactly my secretarial talent, but — please don't think me conceited — my public relations talent. I've always been interested in people, all kinds of people, but now especially the older ones. Add 'lonely' to 'older' and my heart melts.

"My current involvement is with the Northwest Pilot Project, visiting elderly, retired, lonely persons. I try to find some way to bring back a spark of excitement into their long, dreary days. Until you get close to them, Donna, you have no idea how lonely and bereft some Golden Agers are. There's an elderly widower living alone on $165 a month. Sixty-five dollars a month goes for a small, two-room, poorly lighted, poorly ventilated rental. 'When my wife was alive, we used to make do not too badly,' he said, 'but now I'm alone it's — it's——' Tears choked him. Then there's a widow living on $105 a month. 'Half goes for rent,' she says, 'and I hunt around for bargains, but food costs have gone so high, I'm afraid I'll have to apply for welfare. I never have yet, but I guess I'm going to be forced to come to that.'

[1] Geneva G. Moore, *NRTA Journal,* Vol. XX, Issue 95, pp. 60-61.

"When I visit these new friends of mine, I wonder what Browning's verses in *Rabbi Ben Ezra* hold for them:

> Grow old along with me!
> The best is yet to be,
> The last of life, for which the first was made.

It's a poor 'best' that these Golden Agers have. It's pitiful to hear them harking back to 'the good old days.' Here, look at this picture I took the other day. Can't you just see the longing?"

It was several moments before Donna spoke. "This is more than a snapshot. It's a portrait of a universal experience: Yearning for the days beyond recall. Oh, Joan, let me go with you sometime."

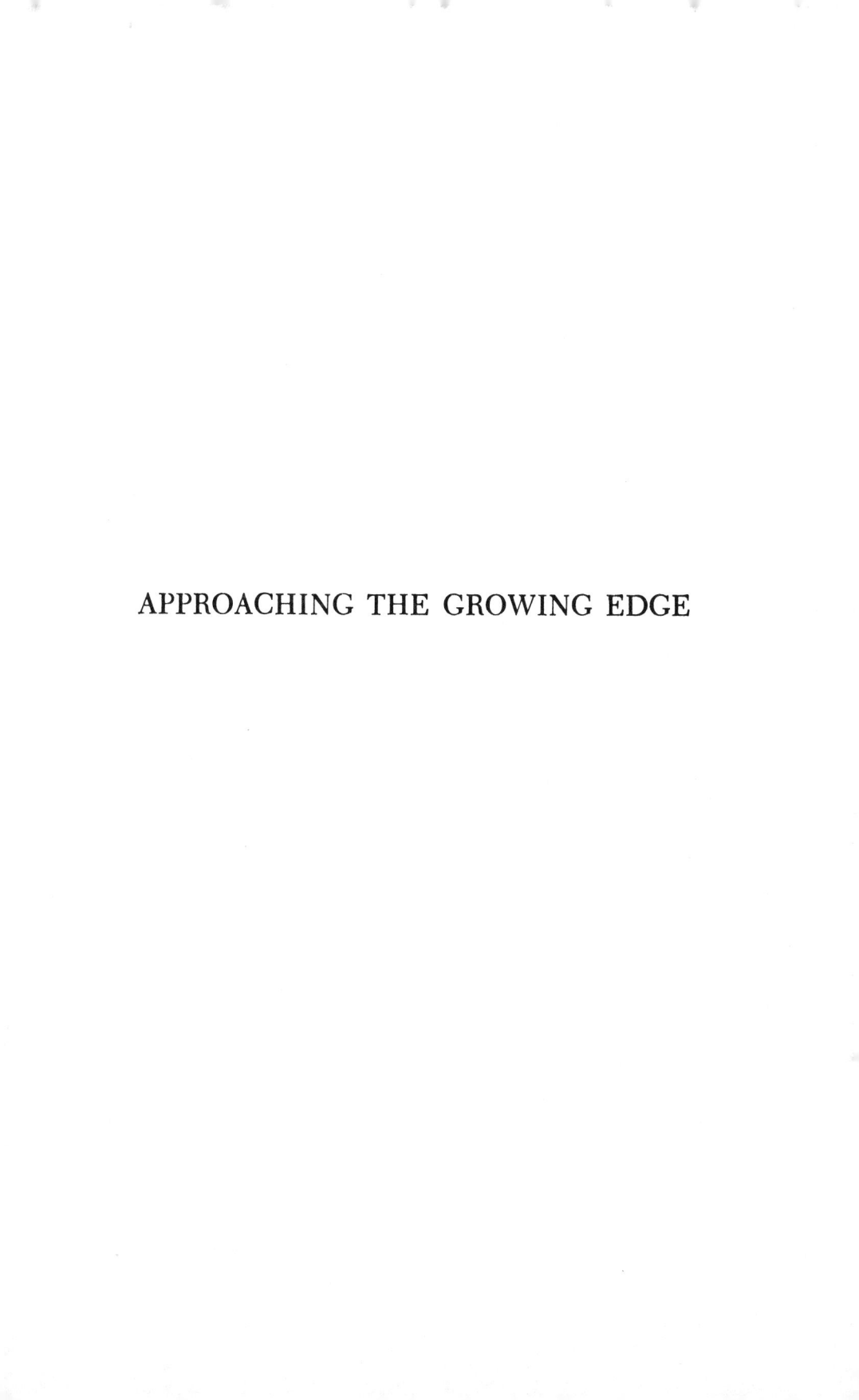

APPROACHING THE GROWING EDGE

3 APPROACHING THE GROWING EDGE

That evening at home, Donna turned to the article "Retirement Is a State of Mind" by Rosalie Harper, who for thirty-eight years had been director of attendance for the schools of her city.

> I categorize myself as an adjusted retiree. . . . Retirement, I believe, is a state of mind. It can be what you want to make it, for you are the key person. . . . You will have many experiences during your first year of retirement; some will be happy and others will be sad. . . . I choose to go on living a rich, full life. . . . If I ever find myself looking backward instead of forward, I will just say out loud: "Pardon me, is my retirement showing?"[1]

"Hm-m," Donna mused, "no hankering for fleshpots there."

But the next week when she went to the Pilot Project with Joan, she heard plenty of hankering. All but one

[1] *NRTA Journal,* March-April, 1970, Vol. XX, No. 94, pp. 56-57.

of the four elderly persons she visited spoke wistfully of the past, how good those days were and how different from these days now. And all but that one had little interest in life except to live through each day; one even said he'd be happier if he didn't last that long. "What is left in life for me anyway?"

The same day that Donna went to the Pilot Project, I had also gone. I wanted to know more about this work of "love, not charity" begun in 1965 by the Greater Council of Churches in Portland, Oregon. Trained volunteer visitors, many of them elderly, were providing a liaison between older, needy, lonely adults and the formal channels of aid.

It was at that day's conference that I met Donna for the first time. When I found that we lived in towns only twelve miles apart and on the same bus line, I said to her, "Come with me for supper. Then I'll drive you home."

That evening we found we had much in common: both widows, she not so long as I; both retired teachers; both now living alone, with all our children settled at a distance. It was one of those times when within a few hours two persons can say, "No longer strangers, but friends."

Donna poured out her heart, giving glimpses of her early reactions to retirement and her recent restlessness. With her permission those experiences have been recorded above. When I sought that permission, Donna laughed and said, "My retirement blues and welcome to them. But," she was quick to add, "beginning today there's going to be a change in the color. I have a goal now. Promise you'll tell about that too."

"A goal? What's your destination?"

Donna waited a moment in thought before she answered. "The best way I can express it is to head towards the growing edge of life and to help others head in that direction. Does that make sense?"

"Yes, indeed it does. But how?"

"I don't know yet, but I'll think of something."

"Towards the growing edge of life!" All who have suffered the shock of tragedy, death, or change that breaks an established pattern of life have to face that challenge. Each moves towards that edge by his own individual route. One may take her first step when she says, "I'd like some Mexican blue glass tumblers"; one while planting seeds in a springtime furrow; another by clasping a young child's hand; and yet another — and this one moves towards the edge fastest of all — when he volunteers to work with and for other people.

That night I saw that Donna had already taken the first step of her journey to the growing edge. The next week I said to myself, "She's wearing seven-league boots," for now she was no longer referring to the "elderly-lonely," but to "my friends." And after her third week I knew she was within stepping distance.

By that time she was making plans to set up the same kind of project in her own town, much smaller than Portland. "For," she said, "the lonely ones are all around us. Every village, town, and city has them—people who need to know that other people care for them and that sixty-five plus is not a dead end.

"The service is a natural for churches. I'm going to urge all the churches in my town to unite in making a survey of the town's shut-ins and lonely ones, then start to train volunteer visitors, set up 'assurance telephone calls' for daily checks, and maybe even plan to deliver one hot meal a day. Once you get people's Concern [the capital 'c' was in her tone] aroused and activated, there's no end to the services the mind and heart will suggest."

Yesterday, just one month from the day I first met Donna, she came for tea. Even before the water had boiled or the cinnamon toast had been slipped under the broiler, she was chanting, "Guess what I made yesterday."

It was plain to see that she was aglow with enthusiasm, full of what Gladys Scott calls "Savor-zest," that "feeling of obligation" about some activity or project that "you get deeply involved in" and which brings significance to your life.[2]

"Guess," she urged me.

"Homemade cookies?"

"Yes, I always make them, but they're nothing to get excited about."

"Bouquets from your garden."

"Those too, of course, but I mean something that will last longer than food or flowers."

"I give up. Tell me before the toast burns."

"These." She handed me several sheets of paper, saying, "At first I thought of making only a short list of simple things that my Pilot friends might do, but ideas came so thick and fast that I ended with this longer list, and it's only a beginning. Now I'm going to take these to the retirees in my town, hoping to prime some enthusiasm. Remember how we used to use a dipper of water to coax deep well water to flow?

[2] *NRTA Journal,* July-August, 1970, Vol. XX, Issue 96, p. 65.

Approaching the Growing Edge

We've quite a group of sixty-fivers in our town now, and some are getting bored with their retirement. Hobbies, I've heard, are better than apples to keep doctors away. No, don't call my town's retirees "Golden-Agers.' They dislike that name. Any suggestions?"

"How about 'Robert Brownings — Pro and Anti'? That'd take in all who agree 'the best is yet to be' and those who think otherwise. The camp is divided, you know."

Then, pushing aside my half-empty cup, I took the sheets on which Donna had listed hobbies in their three categories.

Arts and Crafts

Beadwork (belts, flowers, necklaces)
Brass rubbings (a hobby of the late 1880's, now revived)
Building bird houses
Collages
Decoupage
Doll-making and doll-dressing (Heads from dried apples are fantastic.)
Embroidery
Fun with felt
Jewelry (rings, bracelets, pins, necklaces from agates, beads, buttons, plastic, papier-mache, wood, etc.)
Knitting
Leatherwork
Mosaics (from broken china, buttons, cracked eggshells, seeds, etc.)
Painting
Pottery
Papier-mache (An old art revived for making holiday decorations, jewelry, screens, stack tables, toys, and many other items.)
Quilting
Rugs (braided, crocheted, hooked, woven)

Rocks (polishing)
Sewing (Spread joy from sewing for orphanages, mission stations, refugee centers.)
Shellcraft
Tatting
Wreaths (For Christmas, made of artificial fruit-della Robbia — broken jewelry, buttons, candy wrapped in cellophane, felt, feathers, food, gilt leaves, greens, holly, lace, nuts, paper doilies, pistachio nut shells colored red and formed into poinsettias with mustard seeds for centers, ribbon bows.)

Collecting

Antiques (Of course! Who ever thinks of collecting without thinking first of antiques? Recently a special brand of antiques has come into being: *Junque*, formerly called "junk.")
Bells
Bookmarks
Boxes (Old tin ones are the current fad.)
Coins
Driftwood (small pieces for flower arrangements and conversation pieces; larger ones for garden)
Fans
Glassware (bottles, fruit jars, tumblers. Inquire at public library for books quoting present value.)
Jokes (For a starter: A reporter, interviewing a man on his 100th birthday, asked in kindly humor, "Do you think you'll live to see another hundred?"
 "Can't tell," said the centenarian, "but I'm a lot stronger now than when I started my first hundred.")
Pictures (Group into categories: activities, animals, babies, children, flowers, scenery.)
Quilt patterns
Rocks
Recipes
Stamps
Shells
Superstitions

Approaching the Growing Edge 39

ACTIVITIES

Bird-watching

Cooking (Try new recipes. Great fun!)

Decorating (boxes, pails, wastebaskets, just about anything. See book on Tole painting.)

Entertaining (One or two or ten plus food and games, conversation, and sharing of talents.)

Fishing

Foster Grandma & Grandpa (To give the experience of love to children in hospitals and orphanages.)

Gardening (In any available space — even in large boxes outside the door or in pots on window ledges.)

Jogging (With doctor's permission!)

Living (Just plain, daily, uncomplaining living suggested by this story: After a visitor had urged an eighty-seven-year-old man to become interested in some activity, the octogenarian replied, "Well now, when a fellow's pushing on to eighty-eight, I think that's activity enough. Don't you?"

Music (listening, performing, studying)

Painting

Politics

When I came to this item, Donna said, "Did you see the article in *Parade* titled 'Senior Power Is on the Move'?[3] It's about 'the march of the latest pressure group — senior citizens . . . organizing, demonstrating, demanding, and flashing ballot-box muscle as never before.'"

"Yes, I read the article. 'Ballot-box muscle' — I like the term. We elderly are a 20,000,000-strong new liberation front now. By 2000, when government projections say we'll be 33,000,000-strong, no telling what may happen. Youth beware!"

For a moment Donna and I were silent, lost in our

[3] Theodore Irwin, 13 September 1970, pp. 12, 14.

own private musings. Then I turned back to her listing of activities.

> Puzzles (crossword, jigsaw, dozens of others)
> Reading (alone or aloud to others. Check library for loan of Talking Books.)
> Scrapbooks (for children's hospitals, nurseries, day-care centers, using pictures collected)
> Sculpting
> Studying (adult education classes; correspondence courses, college and university courses open to senior citizens; Institute of Lifetime Learning at Washington, D.C.; and many others)
> Walking (Between ambling and jogging, among the most healthful of all activities.)
> Tutoring (The other side of the "studying" coin.)
> Travel (armchair in front of a T.V. set, books, travelogues, real. Check tours in *Modern Maturity* magazine.)
> Visiting (newcomers, shut-ins)
> Volunteer services (church, "Fish," hospitals, rest homes, wherever needed)
> Writing (articles, autobiography for family, books — oh, yes, you can! — letters, local history, pen pals, poetry, or just a diary)

"Well," I exclaimed when I came to the end, "you're certainly offering a generous and palatable fare of new stews. Little danger that your new friends — or for that matter any retirees — will have time to hanker for the old fleshpots once they dip into some of these savories."

"Oh, I hope so." Donna's eyes were sparkling. "And who knows where a hobby may lead. Start doing something just for the sake of doing and it may turn out to provide a supplement to the social security check, or even be a profitable second career."

When I suggested to Donna that she should have copies of her lists made, she said, "I've already arranged for that. There's a new print shop across town from me. Just a minute. I think I have the card."

After fishing through the contents of her bag, she found the card and handed it to me. I read:

BILL VANCE
Small-job Printer
Retired   —   June 30, 1970
Reactivated — October 1, 1970

"Now there's a retiree who is putting his talents to work," Donna said, "and getting money for it."

"More and more are doing it," I added. "Employment bureaus for the elderly are springing up in many places. *Mature Temps* is already established in New York and Philadelphia and other cities. Southern California has *Experience Incorporated*. And, of course, the President's Committee on the Aging already has older folk in mind in relation to the Economic Opportunity Act. And . . ."

"That's another thing I must get started in my town," Donna broke in, " a local committee to care for our own elderly who need part-time work."

Donna was certainly moving fast towards changing the "blues" of her retirement to springtime "green."

The next week she had not only gotten her lists printed, but had added Bill Vance and his wife Martha to her list of friends, and through her I came to add them, too, to my list. During subsequent reciprocal visitings, Bill shared what he called "early symptoms of retire-itis," some of which are recorded above in the first two chapters.

One day he said, "There should be a symbol on my card — the picture of a vacuum — but I'd get tired telling folks what a vacuum sweeper has to do with my 'Reactivated.'" He winked at Martha.

"Big tease," she murmured, "with the memory of an elephant."

To myself I thought, And the solid footing of one, too. See how quickly Bill has come to *his* growing edge.

Years ago, when my husband and I were visiting his sister on our first furlough after five and a half years in China, our brother-in-law took us to Mount Rainier to see the ski races on the Fourth of July. Skiing on the Fourth! To us it was amazing. But much more amazing was what we saw at the melting edge of the glacier. Nested under a small ledge of crusted snow and honeycomb ice was a growing plant. Two of its white blossoms had pushed out slightly beyond the edge, but one had come up straight through the crust.

Now when I hear people in the winter years of their lives lamenting, "There is no longer a growing edge," I think of those flowers, and I link them to the words that Jesus said about the birds of the air, "Are you not of more value than they?" (Matthew 6:26).

A CLOUD OF WITNESSES

4 A CLOUD OF WITNESSES

After a long list of the faithful, from Abel and Abraham and Sarah to David and Samuel, the prophets, and others (Hebrews 11:4-38), the writer of the "Letter to the Hebrews" begins chapter twelve with this challenge:

> Therefore, since we are surrounded by so great a cloud of witnesses, let us also lay aside every weight, and sin which clings so closely, and let us run with perseverance the race that is set before us, looking to Jesus the pioneer and perfecter of our faith, who for the joy that was set before him endured the cross, despising the shame, and is seated at the right hand of the throne of God.

In all areas of life, witnesses are valuable assets. In case of an accident, they help to determine liability. In case of a false charge against one's character, they help to clear one's name. In case of weakening faith, the mere memory of the faithful can act as a transfusion to bring renewed spiritual strength and raise lagging morale.

In the experience of aging, when occasionally — or is it all too often? — we feel the heavy weight of the years and fall into the sin of despondency and/or boredom that clings so closely, who can better raise our fraying spirits than those who have successfully weathered the years and established their own beachheads on the farther side of the dividing line between the arid and the humid, the barren and the fruitful?

Think now of persons who in the years after their three-score-and-five have run with perseverance their own personal races. At random we note here but a few:

Frank C. Laubach, who at the time of his death in June, 1970, when he was eighty-five, was still working on literacy primers to complete three hundred of them in many languages and dialects.[1]

Grandma Moses, who, between the time she painted her first picture at the age of seventy-six and the time of her death at the age of one hundred and one, had to her credit over a thousand paintings, some hanging in museums not only in the United States but also abroad.

Colonel Sanders, the twinkly-eyed, white goatee-bearded man (at least so pictured in advertisements) of Kentucky Fried Chicken fame, who, after several disappointments, emerged in his later years as a shining example of one who succeeded greatly.

Rose Kennedy, eighty years old in July, 1970, who, having lived through great tribulations, was able to

[1] *Christian Century*, 24 June 1970, p. 782.

say a few days before her husband died, "We have known joy and sorrow. The agony and the ecstasy. And I must be grateful because our triumphs have been greater than our tragedies." Of their tragedies she says, "I am not going to be vanquished by these events. I don't intend to be laid low or pulverized. If I collapsed, the morale of the whole family would be lowered." [2]

Alonzo Stagg, who in 1933, at the age of seventy, left his coaching position at the University of Chicago to coach at the College of the Pacific in Stockton, California; who at the age of eighty was elected "Coach of the Year"; who only in 1961, at the age of ninety-eight, finally retired; and who at his one hundredth birthday party joked: "I may go on forever because statistics show that few men died after the age of one hundred." In March, 1965, he died in his sleep.[3]

Open almost any book on gerontology and you will see reference to persons who have found or are finding that the "leisure years" are anything but leisurely. In *Wake Up Younger!* names and ages hold one's interest:

> At 80, Plato was still at work. Michelangelo remained productive until 90. Titian painted one of his masterpieces at 94. John Wesley was still preaching at 88. Benjamin Franklin's greatest contribution came after 70 when he was tormented by diseases. John Adams, John Quincy Adams, Thomas Jefferson, and James Madison remained busy long after 70. Noah Webster started yet another dictionary at 84. Verdi's greatest operas were composed in his last years.[4]

[2] Pearl Buck, "The Kennedy Women," *Good Housekeeping*, June 1970, p. 171, © 1970 by the Hearst Corporation. Reprinted by permission.

[3] *Time*, 26 March 1965, p. 45.

[4] Samuel Gertman, M.D., and Helen Alpert, The Citadel Press, New York, 1961, p. 242.

Virginia Whitman tells of Roscoe Pound who upon retirement at seventy-seven, as dean emeritus of Harvard Law School, learned a Chinese language, and of Queen Mother Elisabeth of Belgium who started studying Russian in her eighties.[5] Sidney Gamble, grandson of Procter and Gamble, did volunteer work as president of Church World Service. At seventy-four he was traveling here and there overseeing the various projects.[6]

Henry Durbanville quotes a letter to the *Daily Mail* giving results of the survey of over four hundred names of the most noted men in all times, from all activities. It was found that 35% of the world's greatest achievements came between the ages sixty to seventy, 23% between ages seventy and eighty, and 6% in the years after eighty.[7]

"But," I hear objections from all quarters, "I'm not a Laubach and never could be." "I'm not a Rose Kennedy, and a thousand witness transfusions could never make me her equal."

Neither will Bill Vance become a Moses or a Colonel Sanders. Nor will Donna Swanson become a Sarah or a Grandma Moses. Those shortcomings, however, do not justify blowing away the whole cloud. Notice in Hebrews 11 the unnamed to whom the writer pays tribute: "women . . . some . . . others . . . ."

Let us turn now to the "some" and the "others" of contemporary retirees who are not so well-known as those mentioned above. Closer to our own levels,

---

[5] *Around the Corner from Sixty*, Moody Press, Chicago, 1967, p. 50.
[6] *Ibid.*, p. 58.
[7] *The Best Is Yet to Be*, R. McCall Barbour, Edinburgh, 1957, p. 48.

these others may better speak to our conditions; their types of morale may better match ours for a successful transfusion.

Let me first share with you the accomplishments of three of my personal friends. The most recent news of one has come from a front-page article printed in the *San Diego Union* titled " 'Pepper' Cameron Works 25,500 Volunteer Hours."[8] On the "Pink Lady" roster she is listed as Mrs. Harry H. (Florence) Cameron. Seventy-years-old-plus now, she is as peppy as she was in the 1920's when I knew her in China. Widowed in 1969, she continues services for San Diego hospitals at stints of five hours daily which she began twelve years ago. When asked why she devotes so much time in volunteer service, she answered, "Well, I wouldn't want to sit around doing nothing."

Another friend of mine, one from our days at Redlands, California, brings to mind the ancient Chinese proverb, "A journey of a thousand *li* (about 1/3 mile) begins with one step." Edith Parker Hinckley, widow of George Hinckley, began the first step of her graduate journey when she was eighty years old. The end of her thousand *li* trip came in 1965 when she received the degree of Master of Arts in English from the University of Redlands. Her Master's thesis was "The Crimes and Scandals of Early Redlands," "early" referring primarily to the years before 1910.[9]

A third friend, one from more recent years, Grace Bennett, widow of the Reverend James Bennett, received her B.A. degree at the age of seventy. For nine

---

[8] Jeannette Branin, 7 September 1970.
[9] From "Folks in the News," *Modern Maturity*, Vol. 8, No. 5, p. 44.

years while she was head resident of a men's dormitory at Linfield College, McMinnville, Oregon, she had "chipped away" at course requirements. Her eight children, all of whom worked their ways through college, may have been tempted to think that once "mother" set out to follow their footsteps, she'd breeze through, but Grace Bennett says, "You do not remember as well when you're older. You really don't. I had to take a language, so I took Spanish. I put it off until last. It nearly killed me, but I made it." Made not only "it," but also the honor of being Oregon's Mother of the Year for 1969. Her word of witness for us now is "Most people can do a lot more than they think they can." [10]

It isn't only the sixty-five-years-plus women who have a thirst for more education; some elderly men also return to the schoolroom. Robert W. Ross, Sr., is one of them. With more than forty years of teaching behind him, a B.S. degree in education, and thirty hours of graduate credit at the University of Cincinnati, he is now, at the age of eighty-three, enrolled in a calculus course at Ashland Community College, Kentucky. "You never want to let the knowledge get away . . . . You always need to keep in touch with it," he says.

Once a person begins to look for testimony that life is more pleasant if you don't put on your slippers yet, witnesses come from all directions. Yesterday's paper told of Mrs. Elizabeth Morin, a widow, who in 1969, at the age of eighty, started teaching a poetry writing class at Patton State Hospital in California. She con-

---

[10] From "Mrs. Grace B. Bennett: Annuitant Extraordinaire," *Tomorrow,* January, 1970, p. 21.

fesses that she started with "fear and trembling," but now, eighteen months later, with pride and joy she holds a book of poems written by her male students. It was a rare privilege granted her to teach in the maximum security ward but a justified one, for as Lo Verne Brown said after his program of reading from the book, "In her classes, Mrs. Morin holds the door open and lets the sunshine in." [11]

"Great," someone says, "but I'm not a student, and I'm not a poet. What value is there for me in these witnessings?"

So you don't want to study and you say you can't teach. But you can love, can't you? All over the land opportunities are opening up for retired persons to give a little love — and not just volunteer love. The Office of Aging is funding programs called "Love to Share" like the one at Forth Smith, Arkansas. Look at the witness-bearers there. Adults, mostly between sixty-three and sixty-five, after an orientation program, are using their talents to care for "latchkey children." Unnamed and unsung, these older persons are after-school-hours guardians of children whose parents work. They provide a bulwark against emotional problems that might so readily develop for the half-orphans. The rewards, though, are not just for the children. The part-time proxy parents receive, in addition to a check, a sense of worth and satisfaction for having been of real service. In the words of the project director at Fort Smith, "They are retiring *to* life, rather than *from* life." [12]

[11] *The Oregonian*, 29 September 1970.
[12] *Ibid.*, 28 September 1970

In Oregon we have a Green Thumb Program made up of retired rural people, mainly farmers, who through landscaping talent help improve the county and city parks, state highways, historical sites, and community centers. The program involves about two hundred persons working in eleven counties under the supervision of the Oregon Highway Department. These Green Thumbers are paid a weekly salary from a federal grant by the United States Department of Labor which jointly sponsors the program with the National Farmers Union. This year the program received the "Merit Award" of the Soil Conservation Society of America. What satisfaction must have come to those retired folk! And what an example for other communities!

Confining a mini research to the section "People in the News" of the last five issues of *Modern Maturity*, the magazine of the American Association of Retired Persons, we find ourselves surrounded by an engaging cloud of witnesses.

The Cecil Peers, who retired from farming fifteen years ago, now manage the Green Tree Forest, a Christmas tree nursery near Boscobel, Wisconsin. Their shop extends 1,500 acres over Wisconsin's rolling grasslands, where the Peers and fifty helpers cut, trim, and spray their wares.[13]

Mrs. Isabella Coleman of Pasadena, California, designs and builds many of the floats for the Tournament of Roses Parade, a self-imposed duty which she acquired fifty-three years ago when the parade was a new event. She has talked a few times about retiring to let her two sons take over her designing duties, but

---

[13] *Modern Maturity*, Vol. 12, No. 6, p. 47.

new years just keep coming around and she says, "I keep getting new ideas." [14]

For twenty-nine years Laura Watson was known to the patients of Central State Hospital in Milledgeville, Georgia, as "the Christmas card lady." At first she rejuvenated used cards for the patients to use, but later with free-will donations she bought leftover cards from wholesale dealers at a greatly reduced cost. Her steady rate for the ten years before she retired was 20,000 cards a year.[15] The new "Christmas card lady" is now Mrs. Carolyn K. Seivers, who succeeded Mrs. Watson after her retirement.[16]

George F. Grebey, former Marine, football player, amateur heavyweight champion, fruit seller, policeman, and engineering draftsman, has retired to duckpin bowling and painting, mostly religious subjects, for pleasure. He says he's having the time of his life. The seventy-one-year-old Grebey, who used to draw for a living and now draws for fun, regards a painting of the Crucifixion scene as his masterpiece. Grebey says he began to paint as an alternative to visiting doctors' offices with imaginary ailments.[17]

Ninety-six-year-old Philip Racciopa still shines shoes for a quarter. Customers say he gives the best shine in town. He says he keeps working because he feels better if he does something. "If not, I sleep, and that's no good. I need the exercise." [18] (I doubt if *he* even owns a pair of slippers.)

[14] *Ibid.*
[15] *Ibid.*, p. 48.
[16] *Modern Maturity*, Vol. 13, No. 2, p. 43.
[17] *Ibid.*, p. 32.
[18] *Modern Maturity*, Vol. 13, No. 3, p. 50

Mrs. Antha Cranford, over seventy, has hooked over one hundred rugs, no two alike. Her hundred and tenth rug she plans to give to a friend, in keeping with her philosophy of "loving and giving." [19]

Dr. Joseph Jacobs, ninety-one years old, is still a practicing physician. During the last sixty years he has delivered at least 3,000 babies. For the last ten years he has been thinking of retiring, but his wife Frances, eighty-six, doubts that he will. "He can't quit," she said. "He'd be lost." [20]

Earl H. Beshlin recently celebrated his hundredth birthday. "He is believed to be the oldest practicing attorney in the United States . . . ." He remembers the days we didn't have income taxes and the government was financed by levying tariffs. He attributes his longevity to abstaining from tobacco. "I hate tobacco as much as the devil hates holy water." [21]

One of the most heartening stories from my own town is that of the Ewerts — Abe and Sue — who are now in Shaikapur, West Pakistan. Mr. Ewert, a retired plumber, should have been thinking of taking it easy. Instead, when he heard a missionary on furlough from West Pakistan tell of the shortage there of people with just ordinary skills, Mr. Ewert began thinking of what he could do. In a town of 50,000 with only one native plumber, there just might be something he could do. There was. There was also something for Mrs. Ewert — working in the hospital and helping care for the children of the missionaries.[22]

[19] *Ibid.*
[20] *Ibid.*, p. 51.
[21] *Modern Maturity*, Vol. 13, No. 4, p. 49.
[22] From a special feature story by Beth Gunderson, *News-Register*, 30 September 1970.

A Cloud of Witnesses

Going out as short-term missionaries or as teachers of missionary children living in isolated areas, or working in the Peace Corps or in Vista seems now to be "the Thing" for retirees. My friends Dr. and Mrs. W. C. Smith, have spent a year at Piney Woods, and another friend, Mrs. Emma Wingler, is now in Indonesia. In the case of the Ewerts and Emma, their desires to be missionaries, frustrated in their youth, are now being fulfilled in their retirement years.

In California, Will Westfall, now in 1971, ninety-two years old, is still supervising the beautiful gardens at Mount Hermon, the site of Christ-centered camps and conferences for the entire family.

See what a well-shod cloud of witnesses surrounds us. And beyond them are clouds upon clouds. Like the writer to the Hebrews, I too must add, "And what more shall I say? For time would fail me to tell" of the hundreds — the thousands of retired folk who have not yet put on their slippers.

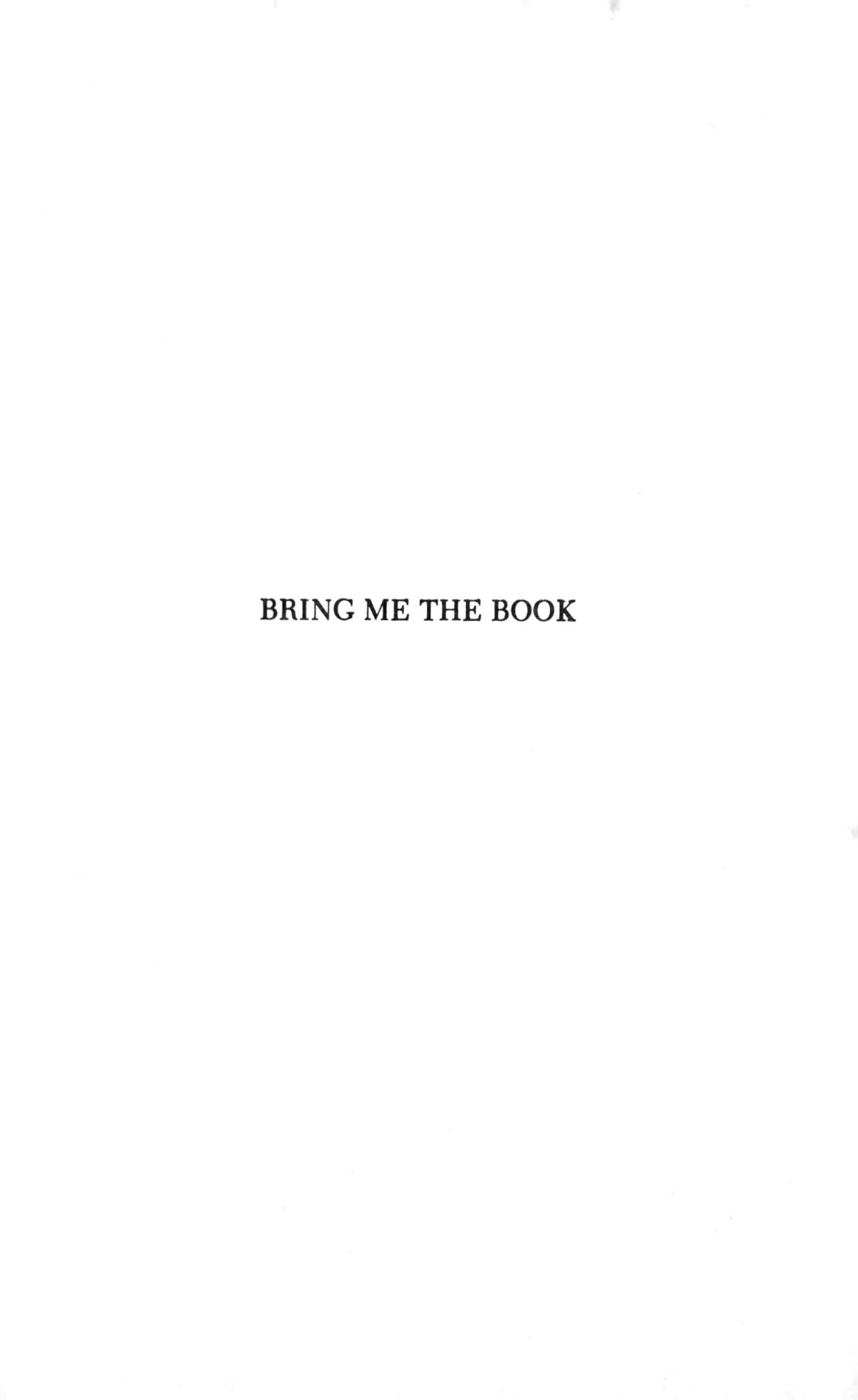

BRING ME THE BOOK

5 BRING ME THE BOOK

Near the close of his "Second Letter to Timothy," Paul makes certain personal requests:

> When you come, bring the cloak that I left with Carpus at Troas, also the books, and above all the parchments (2 Timothy 4:13).

Of this passage, the Reverend William Barclay writes:

> He wants the *books;* the word is "biblia," which literally means papyrus rolls; and it may well be that these rolls contained the earliest forms of the gospels. He wanted the *parchments.* The parchments could be one of two things. They might be Paul's necessary legal documents, especially his certificate of Roman citizenship. More likely they were copies of the Hebrew Scriptures, the Old Testament, for the Hebrews wrote the rolls of their sacred books on parchment made from the skins of animals. It was the word of Jesus and the word of God that Paul wanted most of all when he lay in prison awaiting death.[1]

In the later years of life there come times when, although we are not in prison as Paul was, we want the same books and parchments that he wanted. We

---

[1] From *The Letters to Timothy, Titus and Philemon,* tr. and inter. by William Barclay. Published in the U.S.A. by The Westminster Press, 1961. Used by permission.

wish to review legal documents, check certain records, content ourselves that important papers are in order, and see that our will is clear in all details and legally witnessed. Most of all, though, we want the sustaining, comforting Word near at hand.

What comforts, what strengths does the Book have for the older-than-middle-age? Numberless, yet no person can say one passage strengthens most, for each has his own favorite meadow among the Psalms and his own special resting place "beside the still waters" of Jesus' words.

By-passing favorite personal passages, let us explore a more universal field, asking not "What does the Bible say directly to me as an individual?" but "What does it say about the elderly *per se?*"

We begin with Moses. The symbols of his life — bulrush cradle among reeds of the Nile, rod turned into snake and back to rod, burning bush, plagues for Pharaoh, tablets of stone (two sets), manna in the wilderness — these are too well-known for elaboration. But now comes the time when Moses, aging and exhausted from the heavy responsibilities he has borne, cries out to God. (And what man down through the centuries has not cried out when strains and stresses mount?)

> Why hast thou dealt ill with thy servant? And why have I not found favor in thy sight, that thou dost lay the burden of all this people upon me? . . . I am not able to carry all this people alone, the burden is too heavy for me (Numbers 11:11-14).

And the Lord said to Moses:

> Gather for me seventy men of the elders of Israel . . . and let them take their stand there with you.

> And I will come down and talk with you there; and I will take some of the spirit which is upon you and put it upon them; and they shall bear the burden of the people with you, that you may not bear it yourself alone (Numbers 11:16, 17).

Is this an ancient word of the Lord uttered only for Moses' comfort? Has it not been repeated over and over again for every modern-day exhausted leader *if*, like Moses, he is humble enough to confess his need?

Paraphrased, the passage reads, "Fear not. There are others to take your place," and at its core is the inexorable truth, "No man is indispensable."

Ah, but that is hard to take. No one wants to be dispensable. Yet, we must admit that acceptance of that truth is a mark of the truly mature, the wholly adjusted to life and all its changes.

John LaFarge, S.J., in his book *Reflections on Growing Old*,[2] writes of "Growth Through Diminishment." Had his book been available in the second half of the second millennium B.C., Moses might not have lamented, "Why have I not found favor in thy sight?" Perhaps he could then have seen that the heaviness of his burden was not so much due to the burden as to the diminishing of his own strength, a natural concomitant of aging. And he could have read in it God's favor, not His disfavor, for the writer of *Reflections* considers the diminishing of strength as a sign that the spirit is being made ready for a new planting.

> Is it unreasonble to ask whether this lessening — in a certain way — of the human being is not simply a prelude to, a prerequisite for, a new life of vastly increased power and existence?[3]

[2] Doubleday and Company, Inc., New York, 1963.
[3] *Ibid.*, p. 29.

But, of course, those words could not have been written before Jesus said:

> Truly, truly, I say to you, unless a grain of wheat falls into the earth and dies, it remains alone; but if it dies, it bears much fruit (John 12:24).

So, when the buoyancy of youth lessens and muscles and joints protest, the Reverend John LaFarge would have us take comfort and find excitement in the thought that the eternal part of us is simply preparing itself to be a seedling in some place "eye hath not [yet] seen."

One other experience of Moses is so poignant that I feel tears start each time it is brought to my remembrance. When, near the end of his life, Moses is coming close to the Promised Land, he pleads:

> O Lord God, thou hast only begun to show thy servant thy greatness and thy mighty hand; for what god is there in heaven or on earth who can do such works and mighty acts as thine? Let me go over, I pray, and see the good land beyond the Jordan, that goodly hill country, and Lebanon (Deuteronomy 3:24, 25).

After all Moses had done leading God's people, after all those hard, faithful years, was this request too great? Such a small one — just to set foot on the Promised Land, just to have a taste of the milk and honey, just to see for himself how heavy the grape clusters were on the vines.

> But the Lord was angry . . . and said . . . "Let it suffice you; speak no more to me of this matter. Go up to the top of Pisgah, and lift up your eyes westward and northward and southward and eastward, and behold it with your eyes; for you shall not go over this Jordan (Deuteronomy 3:26, 27).

How many Jordans have we prayed God to allow us to pass over, and how many passings has He refused? Do we lose our faith in a loving Heavenly Father because of His refusal? If we do, why should we? Did we lose our love for our earthly father when he said, "No"? Are faith and love contingent upon permissiveness? If to Moses it was given only to behold the Land with his eyes, who are we to rail if, coming to the end of our lives, we must leave some of our dreams unfulfilled and view some fond hope only from a distant Pisgah?

Next let us consider Rehoboam, the younger-than-middle-aged son of Solomon, who ruled after Solomon's death. At the coronation in Shechem, Jeroboam, who earlier had revolted under Solomon's oppression and fled to Egypt but at Solomon's death had returned from Egypt, now led the assembly of Israel to present their grievances to Rehoboam. Their complaint was that Solomon had laid a heavy yoke on them. Now they promised that if Rehoboam would make their burden lighter, they would serve him.

Rehoboam answered, "Come back in three days." He was buying time to seek counsel. First he went to the old men, asking, "How do you advise me to answer this people?"

The old men said,

> If you will be a servant to this people today and serve them, and speak good words to them when you answer them, then they will be your servants for ever (1 Kings 12:7).

But Rehoboam had no mind to humble himself in this fashion so he sought further counsel — this time from the young men.

"Be tough," they advised. "Thus shall you speak to this people . . . 'My little finger is thicker than my father's loins. And now, whereas my father laid upon you a heavy yoke, I will add to your yoke. My father chastised you with whips, but I will chastise you with scorpions'" (1 Kings 12:10, 11).

The end result? A division in the land. Rehoboam's threat in such "rough" words "precipitated the revolt of his northern and eastern subjects, and Rehoboam fled in his chariot to Jerusalem for safety. Never again was the Hebrew people a united kingdom."[4]

Here is a telling example of what happens when the wise counsel of old men is cast aside for the harsh counsel of hotheaded, arrogant youth. How contemporary the story is! Today all over our country — and the world — there are hotheaded youth counseling and being counseled by other hotheaded youth to "lay it on hard — break, destroy, bomb," while old men plead for restraint, reconciling deeds, and construction instead of destruction.

Now let us see what the Book of books has to say about and for women of advanced years. Straightway Sarah comes to mind. She was old enough to know better than to eavesdrop at the door of the tent when the Lord was holding a private conversation with her husband Abraham. But there she was, and when she heard the Lord saying, "I will surely return to you in the spring, and Sarah your wife shall have a son" (Genesis 18:10), she laughed to herself. "Ha! To me at my age!"

Then God asked Abraham, "Why did Sarah laugh . . . . Is anything too hard for the Lord?"

[4] *Harper Bible Dictionary*, Harper and Row, Publishers, New York, 1954, p. 608.

"Oh," hand to mouth, quickly checking her scornful glee, Sarah said, "I did not laugh."

"But you did laugh."

At present, if the Lord is as greatly concerned about population explosion as His earth-children are, there may not be another Sarah. But there will continue to be times when He will expect the seemingly impossible from the aged — women and men. Then when fear or scorn or disbelief turn us vocal, He will say today what He said to Sarah long ago, "Is anything too hard for the Lord? At the appointed time, I will return . . . and [you] shall——"

Shall what? What will He have planned for us? What will He expect from us? Some task we think beyond our strength? Some sharing that our selfish nature struggles to avoid? Some sacrifice we say would take our life, but instead, when done, brings us new life?

Never think that loaded question, "Is anything too hard for the Lord?" is a one-time query; it is eternal. Like mercy, it drops upon the just and unjust. It spans the widest of generation gaps, often landing more heavily upon the arthritic aged than upon the bouncy young.

Who knows — perhaps it was this very question that Paul reread when the parchments were delivered to him. Surely for a person imprisoned (even though at the time the imprisonment may have been only a house arrest), deserted by Demas, and with Crescens and Titus gone, leaving only Luke, there would be great comfort in a question so patently rhetorical that the answer shines out like a bright star: "Of course, nothing is too hard for the Lord."

Paul had already experienced the truth of that answer.

> At my first defense no one took my part; all deserted me. May it not be charged against them! But the Lord stood by me and gave me strength to proclaim the word fully, that all the Gentiles might hear it. So I was rescued from the lion's mouth (2 Timothy 4:16, 17).

When we are confronted with that question put to Sarah, how blessed we are if we can say with Paul:

> The Lord will rescue me from every evil and save me for his heavenly kingdom. To him be the glory for ever and ever. Amen (2 Timothy 4:18).

Among the many other Biblical characters whose lives have a message for today's aging, we choose for our last two the ones who were in the Temple when Mary and Joseph came for their purification according to the law of Moses (Luke 2:22). One was the man Simeon who

> . . . was righteous and devout, looking for the consolation of Israel, and the Holy Spirit was upon him. And it had been revealed to him by the Holy Spirit that he should not see death before he had seen the Lord's Christ. And inspired by the Spirit he came into the temple; and when the parents brought in the child Jesus, to do for him according to the custom of the law, he took him up in his arms and blessed God and said,
> "Lord, now lettest thou thy servant depart in peace, according to thy word; for mine eyes have seen thy salvation which thou hast prepared in the presence of all peoples, a light for revelation to the Gentiles, and for glory to thy people Israel" (Luke 2:25-32).

Simeon was like "The Quiet in the Land."

They had no dreams of violence and of power and of armies with banners; they believed in a life of constant prayer and quiet watchfulness until God should come. All their lives they waited quietly and patiently upon God. [5]

No need to wonder why Simeon had a revelation from the Holy Spirit; righteousness and devotion are often so rewarded. But without action, the revelation would have died a-borning. Simeon saw to it that it did not die. He did not shrug off the revelation, saying "It's only my imagination." In his youth he might have done this, but through long years of piety he had developed a sensitive awareness to God's leading.

How he could have been certain, we do not know. Each person has his own particular radar. And each has his own terminology. One says, "I had a hunch that was the thing to do." Another says, "God nudged me." Still another, "I just heard God say to me to do this." Such a one was my friend in Redlands, who on the morning of a special anniversary day during my fresh grief invited mother and me to lunch. When I thanked her for such thoughtfulness, she said, "Oh, I didn't know this was a special date. I invited you because during my morning devotions the Lord said, 'Ask Colena and her mother for lunch.'" I did not ask her to describe the voice. Enough that her ears were attuned to divine syllables. It is not the method by which God's message is received that matters; it is the awareness that God has spoken.

And then it is action that makes valid the message. Inspired by the Spirit, Simeon came into the Temple.

---

[5] From *The Gospel of Luke,* tr. and inter. by William Barclay. Published in the U.S.A. by The Westminster Press, 1961. Used by permission.

What a reward awaited him! Think what it must have been to Simeon to hold the Lord Jesus in his arms.

How grateful we should be that then Simeon spoke from his heart, echoing Isaiah 49:6, words that have been preserved for us through the ages in the *Nunc Dimittis* of Christian liturgy!

Notice that for Simeon there was no yearning for "just another year," no sighing, no tears that he was close to the end of his life, no "moaning at the bar." Just a trustful "Now lettest thou thy servant depart in peace," cradled in deep gratitude that his eyes had seen God's salvation for the world. If we can come to the last hour filled with such trust and gratitude, we shall indeed be blessed. At that same time there was Anna, a prophetess,

> the daughter of Phanuel, of the tribe of Asher; she was of a great age, having lived with her husband seven years from her virginity, and as a widow till she was eighty-four. She did not depart from the temple, worshiping with fasting and prayer night and day. And coming up at that very hour she gave thanks to God, and spoke of him to all who were looking for the redemption of Jerusalem (Luke 2:36-38).

Though old in age, Anna was young in spirit. All who look towards the growing edge of life are ageless, and Anna was, without doubt, one of the eager expectants ever gazing towards the fulfillment of prophecies long foretold. To be such a person in that day of Roman domination took courage. The rich and great, the learned and politically powerful held no traffic with hoping for a Messiah. But Anna remained steadfast in her hope.

No matter that Biblical scholars differ in their interpretation of the text — some saying "eighty-four" refers to the duration of Anna's widowhood, others that it refers to her age — the fact remains that Anna had been a widow for a long, long time.

> A widow can know what it is to face a long, lonely and cheerless life, and a solitude made more acute because of the remembrance of happier days. But it was not so with Anna . . . . she did not bury her hope in a grave. . . . In the place of what God took, He gave her more of Himself, and she became devoted to Him . . . and through her long widowhood was unwearying in devotion to Him. She "trusted in God," and her hoary head was a crown of glory (Proverbs 16:31).[6]

Edith Deen, in her comprehensive and beautifully written book *All of the Women of the Bible,* pictures Anna

> as a woman erect for her years, walking about the pillared Temple of Jerusalem in flowing black dress with a shoulder shawl of a brighter hue, probably purple, and paler drapery about her white hair.[7]

Whenever I think of Anna, the widows whom I met in Bethlehem at the Christian Approach Mission come clearly before me. Heavily swathed in black — no shawl of a brighter hue or pale head-drape — they had sat near my daughter and me at the morning service, and later we met them individually during the after-church coffee hour at the minister's house. Economically, theirs is a hard lot, but through their faith in God and in His Son, their Savior, they find a meaning for their lives.

---

[6] Herbert Lockyer, *The Women of the Bible,* Zondervan Publishing House, 1967, p. 30.

[7] *All of the Women of the Bible,* Harper and Row, Publishers, 1955, p. 173.

When we asked to take a picture, the little band gathered at a sunny spot near the fence. Beyond them lay Shepherds' Field, five miles south of Jerusalem. Daily they were within walking distance of each of the places where Jesus is purported to have been born. For them, that which Anna, almost two thousand years ago, "spoke of him" in the Temple had been fulfilled.

Through Anna's watchful waiting and steadfast hope, she won the great privilege and the rare distinction of being the first woman to proclaim Jesus as the Messiah. That distinction was not won by chance; she had earned it.

As Simeon inspires us to trust and gratitude, so Anna inspires us to faithfulness and hope. With her, too, there was no looking back, no sighing, no self-pity that age had displaced youth. It is not at all difficult to think of her as saying, with Simeon, "Now lettest thou thy servant depart in peace . . . for mine eyes have seen thy salvation."

Moses, Rehoboam, Sarah, Simeon, Anna—Paul would have found the first three in the parchments he asked Timothy to bring to him, and more than likely Luke would have had enough of his gospel written by the time Paul was in Rome so that the stories of Simeon and Anna were also available to Paul. With stories like these to review, no wonder Paul asked for his books "and above all the parchments."

With stories like these and a hundred others to strengthen our patience and faith, we would do well to echo Paul's words, saying to our beloved Judy or Mary, Michael or Mark, "When you come, bring me books — above all The Book of books."

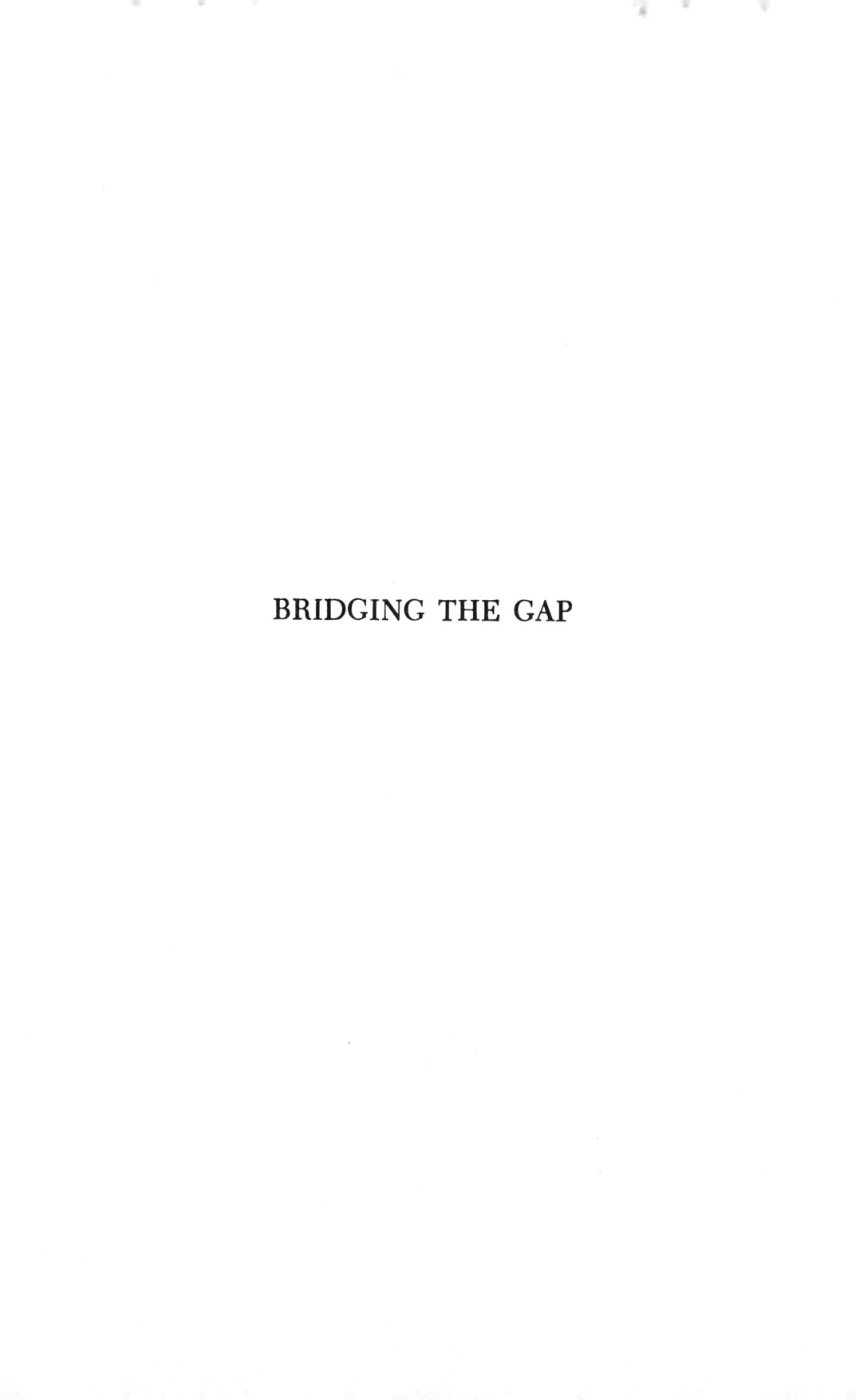

BRIDGING THE GAP

6 BRIDGING THE GAP

Last Friday Donna came for an overnight visit. In the evening we had a nut-cracking party in front of the open fire. As we cracked the shells and picked out the fresh, plump kernels, we talked of the weather, our trips East and South and across the oceans, the Pilot Project, Bill Vance and his small-job print shop—"According to Martha, he's never been so busy and happy."

And then with the fir logs crackling a staccato, we found ourselves tongue-deep in the young generation, making our own crackling sounds about long hair, beads, minis and maxis, and the noise they call music. Donna started describing her reactions to a worship service that the young people had given in her church.

"They had no use for anything traditional. Instead of familiar hymns, they had us singing old folk tunes and some new arrangements. There was one called

'Lord of the Dance' that made me cringe; the imagery was so ghastly. The only instruments used were guitars and drums; not once did they use our lovely, new organ. They ——

"Why are you smiling?" Donna broke her narrative. "What's the joke?"

"No joke," I answered. "I'm just remembering the Sunday morning worship service that our young people gave in our church a few months ago. I spent that whole Sunday afternoon writing my reactions. I wanted them down on paper while they were still fresh in my nerve endings. Want to hear it?"

"Indeed, yes."

So I went to my file, drew out the piece, and read it aloud.

Celebration

The sound of drums came to me while I was yet outside the narthex of our church. Today was the beginning of Youth Week, and knowing that our young people — senior high and college — were to have the service, I was prepared for something different.

But a combo! Beatle music! I was not prepared for that.

Even before I took my seat, I felt a slight squeamishness. With such a beginning, what would the ending be? Two pews ahead of me I saw a dear old friend with her head in her hands, praying, I was sure, that she might endure to that end.

The Prelude went on and on, a plaintive little tune played over and over again, sustained by the steady beat of a drum. There was ample time to read the mimeographed sheet that had been handed to me by the young, coatless, tie-less, long-haired usher — not the usual colored folder with a Scripture verse but an ordinary 8½ x 11 sheet of typing paper headed *Celebration.*

"What a strange name for a worship service," I thought, until I recalled hearing a Catholic friend speak of "the celebration of the mass." "Celebration," of course, "the performance of a religious ceremony," that particular definition of the word familiar to Catholics and Episcopalians — but not to all Baptists. At that very moment how many persons were puzzling over that strange heading so far removed from the traditional "Order of Service"? I was sure I was not the only one.

As the Prelude continued well past eleven o'clock, persons began small conversations with seat-mates. To my own amazement, I, who never whisper in church — well, hardly ever, found myself asking the friend next to me, "Could it be a measure from Bach that they are playing over and over again?"

She raised her eyebrows and answered, "What do you think?"

Think? I was incapable of thinking. All I seemed able to do was feel. The steady beat of the drum was acting like a mixed potion of sedative and stimulant, sedating thought and stimulating emotions.

When the Prelude stopped, I sighed "Thank the Lord" and was leaning heavily against the back of the pew when the combo broke forth again. We were motioned to stand to sing "Joyful, Joyful, We Adore Thee."

"It may be a novel experience to you," the leader said, "to sing this hymn accompanied by drums, but remember that trumpets, timbrels, cymbals, and tambourines were used in the Old Testament temple worship. So why can't we use them?" Of course. Doesn't the 150th Psalm urge us:

> Praise him with trumpet sound . . . .
> Praise him with loud clashing cymbals!

I remembered, too, how David and all the house of Israel had played before Jehovah with harps and with timbrels and with castanets, and that David had once danced with all his might and joined all the house of Israel with shouting. Michal was not at all pleased with David's jubilation.

Even this early in the service, I knew, once the service was over, we'd have many a vocal Michal in our midst. My dear friend two pews ahead would be one of them.

Came now the *Litany of Thanksgiving* (read responsively).

> Lift up your hearts.
> *We lift them up unto the Lord . . . .*
> Make a joyful noise unto the Lord, all ye lands.
> *Serve the Lord with gladness. Come before his presence with thanksgiving . . . .*
> Be thankful unto him, and bless his name.
> *For the Lord is good; his mercy is everlasting; and his truth endureth to all generations.*

Dear familiar words. The echo of the drumbeat in my pulse died away. But then came:

> i thank You God for most this amazing
> day: for the leaping greenly spirits of trees
> and a blue true dream of sky; and for everything
> which is natural which is infinite which is yes
>
> (i who have died am alive again today,
> and this is the sun's birthday; this is the birth
> day of life and of love and wings: and of the gay
> great happening illimitably earth)
>
> how should tasting touching hearing seeing
> breathing any — lifted from the no

of all nothing — human merely being
doubt unimaginable You?

(now the ears of my ears awake and
now the eyes of my eyes are opened)[1]

Free verse by E. E. Cummings with its inferiority — or is it superiority — complex small "i," always offensive to me. To place this modern verse in juxtaposition to the "old and tried and true"! What were our young people trying to do? Shock us?

After the *Litany* came the *Anthem*, "The Lord's Prayer," sung antiphonally (Twentieth Century Folk Mass) with a silent choir pantomiming the prayer as the American Indians do. Although decidedly different from our regular anthems, this was quite understandable, well-done, and a pleasant change.

I relaxed — normalcy was returning — only to be shattered the next moment by four guitarists in plaid sport shirts taking predetermined places on chairs in the outer aisles to add their twanging to the *Hymn for Reflection*. This hymn was a sea chantey about Jonah. It evidently goes over at camp meetings, but here in a formal Sunday morning worship service it stood out like two sore thumbs.

Drum, guitars, plaid shirts, modern verse, and now a sea chantey. How far were the young people going to take us? And how much more was I going to be able to take? I'd take my cue from my friend two pews ahead. As long as she could stand it, I should also be able to stand it; but as soon as she'd leave, I'd leave too.

[1] Copyright © 1950 by E. E. Cummings. Reprinted from his volume *Poems 1923-1954* by permission of Harcourt Brace Jovanovich, Inc.

After the sea chantey came *Readings*.

> The Former Prophets (from the Old Testament)
> The Modern Prophets (from contemporary literature)
> The Prophet (from the New Testament)

In the readings from the Old Testament and the New, I caught only a word here and there, for the voices of the speakers were either too weak or our loudspeaker system was on a temporary vacation. But from the few words I did hear, I was able, through memory, to fill in the others not heard.

Not so with the reading from contemporary literature. All of that was lost to me: author, title, text. And during that period of lostness, I fretted and fumed to myself. Why bring in contemporary prophets? Selections from the Old Testament and the New were enough for our forefathers. Weren't they enough for us?

But then — young people — they were always after some new thing. "Itching ears" — the phrase leapt to my mind. Somewhere in one of the epistles there was a warning against such ears. Had our young people worked with itching ears when they fashioned this morning's program? Or — I felt tolerance breaking through my fretfulness — were they only seeking some new way to express an old truth?

That alternate question brought to mind the furor raised half a century ago by the deacons of the Swedish church in Evanston, Illinois, where my husband was serving as student pastor during the first year of our marriage. At that time we were both students at the University of Chicago: he was studying for his Ph.D. in Education; I for my M.A. in Religious Education.

For a certain Sunday evening service, Elam planned to speak about King Gustav V of Sweden, who so recently had taken a stand for neutrality in the war later to be known as World War I. A timely topic for 1917, Elam thought; and I thought, a fine opportunity to try some new way to announce a meeting. So while Elam labored over his sermon, I labored over a poster. When both were finished, each of us heartily approved of the other's work. On Wednesday night after prayer meeting, Elam carefully mounted the poster on the bulletin board. A timely topic well-advertised.

Sunday morning, eager to show me "how fine the poster looks on the board," he hurried me from the El to the church. "See for yourself," he said.

See what? The bulletin board was empty. But not Elam's office. There deacons, six-strong, were waiting for him, the torn poster in hand. What did Herr Pastor mean putting up such a colored poster on the church bulletin board?

"We all like you," one deacon said, "but this thing that you did — that makes you look like a whippersnapper. And we wouldn't want a whippersnapper for a pastor, so be careful in the future."

"And," said another, "if you want to preach on royalty, preach on King David." At which I had to bite my tongue not to say, "But King Gustavus wouldn't put a woman's husband in the fore of battle to have him killed so that he could marry the widow, and King Gustavus never danced naked in the street."

With this memory as a background, I regretted now that I had not been able to hear the reading from a contemporary prophet. Had I heard it, I might have found it was about some contemporary King Gustavus. Here was a strong warning to go slow on my criticism.

When the sermon began, I reached for the pencil

in the rack in front of me. Better take a few notes on the sermon. But before I put the pencil to work, my heart went out to the young preacher standing there before our heterogeneous congregation: country folk, city folk, merchants, teachers — from kindergarten teachers to college professors to college president, mechanics, research scientists — you name them, we have them. Brave young fellow. Were his knees shaking as mine shook the first time I stood before a congregation? Empathy slowed my pencil.

The young preacher was saying, "Worship without worldly service is meaningless." Wrenching myself from empathy and memories, I put my pencil to work and embroidered the margin of the program with abbreviated notes. "A need for recognizing honesty." "Associate fully with the world." (What did he mean?) "Synchronize the church's calendar with the world's calendar." (Probably read the article about a worship service on Thursday night to take the place of the Sunday morning service.) "The poor in our county." Yes, of course, "The poor you have with you always." But this was not what he was saying. He was talking about outcasts of society.... Homosexuals .... (Hold on, young preacher. Don't you see my dear friend shaking her head? Haven't you heard her say, "I'm sick of that word. Can't turn around without hearing it or seeing it in print.")

Had I not jotted down these notes, I am certain I would not now be remembering as much of that sermon as I do remember. The young man spoke so fast (all young people speak fast, run fast, drive fast) that I missed a great part of his sermon. I wished he'd repeat the quatrain with which he ended. It was something about a babe born in a manger and because of that birth "I can dance with a stranger." Very definitely a plea for brotherhood, but what a jolting way to say it, especially to those of the older and oldest generations in the congregation who say, "I don't dance period." Now if that last line had been "I can talk to a stranger," or "I can eat with a stranger," or, especially for my friend two pews ahead, "I can knit a sweater for a stranger" (she has knit hundreds for strangers), the point of brotherhood would have been much more pertinent and wholly palatable.

When the offering plate was passed, I was tempted to hold it overlong. Here was something warmly familiar to tie me to the past and assure me that I was in "an old accustomed place." But, of course, I had to hand the plate down the line.

And so I entered the period of *Intercession and Confession* with no pacifier, no defense against whatever new onslaught might come from our youth. The program instructed us to respond to the liturgist by saying, "Lord, have mercy upon us."

Successively, from each of the four quadrants of the room, young persons rose to read a news item from that day's newspaper. "Viet Nam." I heard the name, but the speaker was turned from me, so I missed the news. No matter, the overflow of my own heartache over the war there made my heart pour itself out in the response, "Lord, have mercy upon us."

The other readings by the liturgists were headed "Spain," "The South," "Our Local Community." These headings were clearly understandable, but again, because of weakness of voice or the position of the reader, much of the news itself was lost to me. So current, however, was news from these areas that I was already aware of the tensions and hardships. Had the young people been reading in foreign languages, the geographic names alone would have drawn from me the same fervent, deep, "Lord, have mercy upon us."

When was the last time a liturgy had moved me so deeply? I could not remember. I only knew that in those moments our young people were providing me with a liturgy that in meaning and significance surpassed all the printed liturgies I had ever met.

So it was that all my fretting, irritation, and criticism were washed away in the flooding cry for mercy, and I came to the close of the service, *Hymn for Authentic Living*. A strong feeling of oneness with my fellow worshipers swept over me as my voice joined theirs in singing "Blowin' in the Wind." My soul was caught up in the awesome wonder of corporate worship — caught up into one of the highest levels of such worship that I have ever experienced.

In the short, silent moment that followed, I sent up a prayer of thanksgiving for the young people of our church who, having led me through that gamut of mixed and unworthy emotions, had brought me to this place of worship, high and lifted up, where with fellow worshipers, whether or not they were as keenly aware of it as I was, I was affirming the truth of:

> The wind blows where it wills, and you hear the sound of it, but you do not know whence it comes, or whither it goes; so it is with every one who is born of the Spirit (John 3:8).

After the *Benediction* I slowly, carefully folded my program, slipped it into my pocketbook, and left the church with moist eyes.

WHEN DEATH STEPS IN

7 WHEN DEATH STEPS IN

Before another Friday had dawned, letters from three distant towns brought me news of the deaths of old friends. Now there were three new widows who needed comfort.

Some years ago after my husband's sudden death, I wrote a series of letters "To those who truly loved and now freshly mourn." Gathered into booklet form, the small volume bore the title *When Death Steps In,* taken from the poem that our daughter, Frances A. Gulick, wrote for the folder at her father's memorial service:

> I used to wonder if life changed
> When Death stepped in and disarranged
> The pattern of our work and love.
> Now I know. Around, above,
> Life pulses strong, for he is here.
> His goal in life remains as clear

Within our hearts. He is as dear.
And still today, when joy grows dim,
He comforts us as we do him.

A few years ago I condensed the letters into an article that I called "To Keep a Heart From Sinking."[1] It was a copy of this article that I sent to my three friends who were now beginning their widowhood. Because there are, no doubt, readers of this book who are now beginning years without a dear one's physical presence, or are already well along in those years, I feel constrained to share the article with you.

To Keep a Heart From Sinking

That August evening, gazing across the table at my husband, I thought I had never seen him looking so well, so relaxed, so full of *joie de vivre*. The eighteen holes of golf at Riverside that afternoon must have been good for him.

The next morning when I awoke, he was dead.

"Heart," the doctor said. "He never knew what struck him."

But I knew what struck me: a blow so devastating it caused the bottom to drop from my life.

Elam and I had been married for twenty-eight years. Just a few days ago he had said, "It seems more like twenty-eight weeks."

"With three children?" I'd bantered. "Two married and the youngest already eighteen!"

"Even so." He drew me close.

Now he was gone. Our mutual joys, our plans for

---

[1] In 1967 this article won a prize in the *Writer's Digest* Article Contest. In November, 1968, *Christian Herald* published it under the title "Alone."

the future, our happy anniversary dates together, our way of living — all gone beyond return.

True, I still had my children and mother to comfort me, but they, too, were saying, "Gone."

Gone. Even the roof over my head was gone, literally gone, for the house we had been living in during the past six years was the president's house at the University of Redlands.

With the roof went also my vocation. (The wife of a college president soon discovers that the responsibilities and privileges falling to her are not merely avocational; they approach the dimensions of a career.)

So there I was, with every item in the countdown plunging my heart deeper and deeper into a bottomless pit, and all the while knowing that I would have to find another place to live.

The president was dead. His widow would have to move.

But where? The only shelter we owned was a log cabin on forty acres of timberland up in Oregon. All the houses we had ever lived in, except the apartment that first year of our marriage when we were graduate students at the University of Chicago, had been a part of Elam's posts: the missionary and American school houses in Shanghai, China; the president's house at Linfield College; and this house at the University of Redlands.

Appalled by reports of rapid turnover in rentals, I decided to buy. Before I signed the deed, though, I asked a friend to check the construction.

"One of the best constructed houses in town," he reported. "Steel lath under the stucco. Built-in copper screens at all the windows. Steel sash. Joists extra close together." At the door, on his way out, he paused. "And, oh, I almost forgot. It has seven extra bags of cement under the fireplace to keep it from sinking." (In that town some hearths, not so well-structured, had been known to sink.)

Extra cement under a hearth to keep it from sinking. If only there were some extra undergirding, beyond the comfort of one's family and friends, to keep a heart from sinking!

The wish possessed me. But not until after I had returned from Elam's interment in the East did I realize that there was such cement. In fact, two bags had already been poured. Without them, how could I have gone dry-eyed through the memorial service in the crowded chapel of the university, and two weeks later journeyed alone across the continent taking Elam's remains for burial in the cemetery at Orchard Park, New York? How could I have done that without some structuring under my heart?

As I pondered this question, I realized that a special kind of anesthetic had carried me through the strain and stress of those first days. It was as though, at the time of my creation, some benumbing drug had been implanted with a trigger to respond to the pressure of shock and deep grief. Since then I have seen this same anesthetic operating in other lives. When people say, "How could Mary be so calm? Why didn't Joe weep?" I answer, "They were in the anesthesia of grief."

Another "bag," poured years ago, was my own personal faith in life after death. The first part of the fourteenth chapter of John had long been my favorite Scripture:

> Your minds must not be troubled; you must believe in God, and believe in me. There are many rooms in my Father's house; if there were not, I would have told you . . . .[2]

(Although I am used to the traditional "Let not your hearts be troubled," I prefer this version's "rooms" over the older "mansions.")

How many times had I used those verses to try to comfort one bereaved! Now they must comfort me. Thinking of Elam in one of those other "rooms" brought a quickening, and at those moments I definitely felt my heart undergirded.

For only those periods, though, for the finality of death would come pressing in to threaten the foundation. Never to see him again in the flesh. . . . Never to feel his arms around me. . . . Never. Never again.

I was unpacking a box of books when a friend came. "Glad to see you working. Work will help you forget."

Forget death! How can anyone forget the death of a loved one?

While my friend remained, I managed to control myself, but as soon as she left, the flood came. The titles of the books blurred, and the covers became stained with tears. Wiping the drops from one thick volume, I remembered it as the book containing Sir Edward Arnold's *The Light of Asia*. In this long poem he tells the story of the young Hindu mother who came with her dead baby in her arms — although at the time she did not realize it was dead — to beg of the Lord Buddha a remedy to make her baby well.

[2] *The Bible*, An American Translation, University of Chicago Press, 1938, p. 102.

I riffled the pages until I found the place. Buddha said:

> ... find
> Black mustard-seed, a tola; only mark
> Thou take it not from any hand or house
> Where father, mother, child, or slave hath died;
> It shall be well if thou canst find such seed.

And she, after searching, returned to lament:

> I went....
> But when I asked ... they said:
> "O Sister! What is this you ask? the dead
> Are very many, and the living few."

> "My Sister! thou hast found," the Master said,
> "Searching for what none finds — that bitter balm
> I had to give thee ... today
> Thou know'st the whole wide world weeps with thy woe;
> The grief which all hearts share grows less for one."[3]

For a long time I sat there tailor-fashion on the floor, books all around me, the thick volume open on my lap. The past days I had been crying within myself, "Why did Elam have to die? Why? He was too young to die. Only fifty-four."

Now I saw that long-ago, faraway Hindu woman, "dove-eyed, young, with tearful face and uplifted hands," and all about her other mourning mothers, widows, widowers, orphans.... The whole, wide weeping world crowded close, and in the transfusion of griefs there came a strange, inexplicable comfort and strength.

There came, too, an undergirding of my heart

---

[3] Printed in Lin Yutang, *The Wisdom of China and India*, Random House, New York, 1942, pp. 444-445.

When Death Steps In

through prayer, the intercessory prayers of friends for me and the comfort of my own personal prayers. I am a Protestant, belonging to a church that has no "Prayers for the Dead." But I made up my own, and one night I wrote:

> Why should my heart not pray for you
> Now gone from sight but yet to love so dear?
> Before you died I always prayed,
> Although at times you were not near.
>
> Has Death the power now to change
> The current of my heart at last?
> Is faith so weak that it must yield
> Itself to atheistic fast?
>
> Within the frame of God's own love
> You live and move and have your being still.
> No force can mute my prayers that bear
> Your name nor ever will.

And gratitude — what a full "bag" that proved to be! For weeks I had cheated myself of the strength that comes from being grateful. Too full of grief over what was gone, there was no space for thankfulness for what I once had had. Then one Sunday, an anniversary date for Elam and me, the minister prayed before the offering:

> And, Lord, now among Thy other blessings, give us the gift of gratitude.

Seldom have I heard such a short prayer; never have I had a prayer answered so instantaneously.

The gift came to me as the tongues of flames must have come to the waiting apostles. Had I not been in church, I would have stood to sing praises to the Lord for all His benefits: for the years Elam and I had had together, for the freshness of the lovely memories of anniversary dates that matched today's, for the love that still bound us close, for our children. and for a hundred other blessings.

As gratitude flowed out from deep within me, I felt a thing firming under my heart, and from that structure emerged a growing edge of life. All day I seeded that edge with gratitude; with each seeding the edge grew broader and greener.

Even today, many years later, I occasionally have need to pray anew for this gift of gratitude. And each time I pray, the gift comes swiftly in full measure, and the green turf on the growing edge thickens.

Another "bag of cement" that, early in my widowhood, kept my heart from sinking came from a file of poems labeled "These have brought me comfort." Among them was one by Mary Hall:

> If I should die and leave you here awhile
> Be not like others, sore undone, who keep
> Long vigil by the silent dust and weep.
> For my sake turn again to life and smile,
> Nerving thy heart and trembling hand to do
> That which will comfort other souls than thine.
> Complete these dear unfinished tasks of mine,
> And I perchance may therein comfort you.

Elam had often said, "When I retire from the presidency, I'd like to teach." Soon after his death, the challenge to complete his unfinished dream sent me back to Claremont Graduate School to begin working for a doctorate in Far East Studies, that I might be better prepared for teaching. Two years later I was on the faculty of Linfield College. In the classroom I have always felt that I was teaching not just for my-

When Death Steps In

self but also for Elam. And great indeed has been the comfort therein.

So, through the undergirding of my heart with the pouring of these six bags of spiritual cement — nature's anesthetic, faith, empathy, prayer, gratitude, vicarious service — I discovered that the bottom of my life had *not* dropped out.

But still, even now, whenever I dwell on the silence after death, I feel the foundation quake. The gap of communication between the living and the dead is, I know, faith's last proving ground. It is also faith's perpetual siege. Against its onslaught I have built up my own defense stemming from something our physicist son Victor told Elam and me when he came on a short vacation from Oak Ridge, Tennessee, the year before Elam died.

"My mouth is closed now," Victor said, "but if ever I'm allowed to tell what we're doing at Oak Ridge, you'll be surprised. You'll find it hard to believe."

When my first encounter with the Silence came, I found strength in Victor's words. I said then, "If man, for his purposes, can set a seal on other men's lips, why not accept the right of God, for His purposes, to set a seal on lips after death?"

And then my mind carried the analogy further. At the time that Victor spoke, I knew that even if he could tell what they were doing in Oak Ridge, I would not be able to understand; his scientific vocabulary was beyond me. So even if communication between the living and the dead were possible, would I be able to comprehend the messages? Isn't there a new vocabulary for new experiences?

For most of my days this simple bit of philosophy

suffices, but every once in awhile the longing to see, to hear, to touch comes like a tidal wave threatening to wash away the foundation under my heart. At such times I have to get down on my knees to check for cracks in the cement. Finding them, I pour another bag or two of well-mixed prayers and gratitude—and wait.

THE FIFTH BLESSING

8 THE FIFTH BLESSING

When we were in China, we became familiar with the traditional fivefold, good luck wish known as *Wu Fu* (Five Blessings). At our departure for the States, Chinese friends and servants at the university set matches to long strings of red firecrackers and called out "*Wu Fu, Wu Fu!*" (Long life, wealth, rank [we call it "status"], love of virtue, and a peaceful passing from the earth!).

What a full basket of wishes! We Occidentals are lavish with the first four. At birthdays we say "Many happy returns of the day," one way of saying "long life." Always we wish for our friends a raise in salary and position. As for "love of virtue," we're satisfied with a simple "Be good." But "a peaceful passing from the earth" — who would ever say that aloud? Even though, secretly, we wish that for every last friend —

and we should for strangers too—the wish never passes our lips.

In 1789 Benjamin Franklin wrote to M. Leroy:

> Our Constitution is in actual operation; everything appears to promise that it will last; but in this world nothing is certain but death and taxes.

For years the last part of that statement has been a household phrase. The stream of talk about taxes is never below flood-level, and the talk about death is equally that high — that is, death by murder, by highway accidents, by undeclared war. But how vocal are we to our friends about their deaths, and — for this is the theme of this chapter — how often do we speak of our own death?

There is, of course, danger in being obsessed with the "final hour," as there is danger in any other obsession, but by shutting our mind, closing our eyes, and playing ostrich — head in sand — can we make death take a detour around us? In the last chapter of *Your Rewarding Years*, Mrs. Hamilton maintains that our attitude of postponing contemplation of our own death is "rooted in the body's will to live," a strong ally for keeping one's health. So it is that the one experience which is bound to come to each of us

> is the one for which most of us make no conscious preparation. [Yet] the way we look forward to death has a great deal to do with the happiness of our later years.[1]

These words bring to mind the aged Chinese farmer who, years ago, detained my husband and me on our Sunday afternoon walk through his village adjacent to

---

[1] Bobbs-Merrill Co., Inc., New York, pp. 196-197.

the compound of the University of Shanghai where we lived and taught. After the customary greetings — we, "Have you eaten?"; he, "Already have eaten" — he beckoned us into his thatched, mud-floor hut.

"*Kon-i-kon* (Look-see)!" He pursed his lips towards one corner of the room, a chuckle in his voice. It took a moment for our eyes to adjust to the dimness of that corner. Then, as sight cleared, we saw the object of his enthusiasm: a black lacquer coffin.

"Yesterday my son bought this for me. Such a good, filial son! Now I have no further needs or cares in life."

Gruesome to have an empty coffin in the house? Not for aged Wang. For him it was a comfort, a security for his spirit's well-being. In a way, funeral directors here in the States are offering a similar comfort, but only partial, because while they contract to care for the body, they promise no contentment for the spirit at the time of passing. Through funeral service policies they allow us only to choose our own style of coffin, which they then will keep for us; no need for us to keep it in our homes.

In subscribing to such a policy, we try to make arrangements for our funeral easier for those who are left to attend to the last rites. But let us be truly thoughtful of those loved ones. Beware, lest in our attempt to make things easy we make things harder, as did a friend of ours, an ex-seminary president who had "taken care of everything." Telling us of the funeral, one son lamented, "It grieved us and really shamed us to find that father had chosen such a plain, cheap coffin. We wanted one of mahogany, but the mortician had father's wish in writing. What could we do?"

Preparation of this kind and life insurance may satisfy our ego — "Want to be independent to the end. Don't want to burden the family. Want everything in order." Outward order, yes. But how about inner order? Are we as thoughtful of our own spirit's ease as we are of the ease for our loved ones? The question here is not about our soul's salvation (that, we trust, is assured), but about our inner steadiness at the time of death. What preparations do we make for our private emotional security to carry us through that last hour with calmness — yes, even with joy and great anticipation? Are we now fortifying ourselves with trust and faith, confidence and assurance for that greatest of all adventures — passing from this world to the next?

"A peaceful passing from the earth." Does that mean an easy death? No pain, no struggle, no agony? We know that not all deaths are painless. In spite of the advances in medical science, there is no guarantee that death will be physically peaceful. But, protests of frail body notwithstanding, there are preparations we can make for the peaceful passing of our spirits.

From several sides I hear the plea, "Let's not talk about that yet." Not talk about it when our lives are now coming closer and closer to the passing? All crises are more easily handled if one has given forethought to them. "What do you do when——" heads the list of helps for many emergencies: What do you do when your child has a convulsion? What do you do when someone faints? What do you do when you are burned?

In the last chapter we considered what to do when a loved one dies. In this chapter we shall consider what to do as we contemplate our last hour.

Still comes a plea, "Let's not talk about it." But hear John LaFarge asking, "Why not talk about death?" And listen as he reminds us how for weeks before we take a trip, we gather maps and travel folders, we recall the names of relatives and friends who are in the countries or areas we plan to visit, and we become excited at the thought of renewing contact with them. "Why," he asks, "shouldn't we do the same about the greatest journey of all? It is curious that our customs and folklore seem to conspire against such a type of conversation." Curious, indeed, that magazines and books and newspapers and TV programs "feature every kind of death-dealing violence ... but they are reluctant to discuss the simple act of life's termination." [2] And what is said here of mass media can also be said of our own conversations.

So now let us consider some questions concerning death — our own death.

1. *Are we reluctant to leave this earth?*

For all of the shadows and sorrows, burdens and heartaches, we may come at the end to see how much more abundant have been the goodness and joys, the blessings and beauty, and we shall strain to hold them, clinging desperately to life.

In part I know that feeling. It came on strong one day soon after my thyroid operation. I was at that stage of convalescence when the slightest approach to tears cramped my throat. That afternoon my friend Thelma Dolan phoned. "It's such a lovely day, wouldn't your mother and you like a little ride out into the country? The autumn colors are beautiful."

[2] *Reflections on Growing Old,* Doubleday and Co., Inc., New York, 1963, p. 134.

"Beautiful" was an understatement. All the maples were amber and gold, and all the vine maples and poison oak were rubies and garnets. As we turned a corner leading down to a peaceful valley, east and west the encircling hills were ablaze with autumn colors. The utter beauty sent a spasm to my throat.

Inwardly I began to wail, "Oh, and to think I might have died and all this beauty would have——" Before my cry was completed with the words "been lost," clear and strong came a rejoinder, "But since this world holds so much beauty, will not the next world hold much more?" So clear and strong, it was as though someone close by had said the words. Then I knew. Out of the burning bushes east and west, God Himself had spoken. With that my throat relaxed, my whole being filled with joy, and my heart sang with expectancy.

2. *Do we fear the experience of death?*

Then hear Henry Legler in his book *How to Make the Rest of Your Life the Best of Your Life* telling the poignant story of his friend who knew he was a terminal case. The friend faced the situation stoically; Mr. Legler, sorrowfully and prayerfully. One night he came across a passage in Joshua Loth Liebman's book *Peace of Mind* which he felt constrained to share with his friend.

The friend said, "You know I'm not a religious guy."

Mr. Legler said, "This isn't religion. It's just— well, I wouldn't know how to describe it. Let me read it out loud."

> We are like children privileged to spend a day in a great park, a park filled with many gardens and play-

grounds and azure-tinted lakes with white boats sailing upon the tranquil waves. True, the day allotted to each one of us is not the same in length, in light, in beauty . . . . but there is enough beauty and joy and gaiety in the hours if we will but treasure them. Then for each one of us the moment comes when the great nurse, death, takes man, the child, by the hand and quietly says, "It is time to go home. Night is coming. It is your bedtime, child, on earth. Come, you're tired. Lie down at last in the quiet of the nursery and sleep. Sleep well. The day is gone. Stars shine in the canopy of eternity."

Now the end was imminent. A few days before death came, the friend said to Mr. Legler, "It's time to go home. Night is coming."[3]

3. *Do you dread leaving loved ones?*

This is a question that haunts many of us. Even though we long to be united with those who have gone before, we cling to those on earth. "How can I leave thee? How can I part from thee?" are not phrases from a song. They are the heart-cries of a person loving and beloved.

One day so pressing was that dread for me, I previsioned my own death. Then, working my way through the vision, at my arrival I found a new dimension to the experience. The comfort that came to me there I trust will pass on to my children and friends. And to you, too, who may be laboring under that heavy apprehension.

Words are often inadequate vessels to hold a visionary experience, but I could not rest until I had at least tried to capture something of the essence. The verses are still without a title, but I share them with

---

[3] Pocket Books, New York, 1970, *passim* pp. 126-128.

you now, hoping they may lessen whatever dread of parting that may be burdening you.

> The hour of my translation
> From earth's accent to cadence otherwise
> Will come, I trust, as gently as does sleep;
> But if not, still I pray you will not weep
> Too long amid the cypress gloom.
>
> Instead, come close in thought and faith
> To greet foregathered kin,
> And roam the meadows blue,
> And see from out our Father's home
> How pleasant is the vista from my room.
>
> Then live the years ahead in joy,
> And know the word is true
> That love can never lose its own,
> For where I shall have gone
> You will come homing too.

4. *Do we fear the unknown?*

Three helps come to mind. One is from a passage in Harry Emerson Fosdick's *Assurance of Immortality*. For over fifty years, during each of a number of personal physical crises, the image in that passage has sustained me and cast out fear of the unknown. Hear it now:

> An unborn child, even though he were a philosopher, would have no easy time making clear to himself the facts of our earthly life. He lives without air; how can he live with it? He never saw light; how can he conceive it? He is absolutely dependent upon the cherishing environment in which he finds himself, and he cannot well imagine himself living without it. The crisis of birth would seem like death to an unborn child . . . .[4]

[4] Association Press, New York, 1918, pp. 44-45.

The Fifth Blessing

But we know how much fuller life on earth is than life in the womb. By analogy, then, can we not believe that life in the next world will be fuller than life in this world?

Each time I think of Dr. Fosdick's words, a certain comparison comes to mind: What the lungs of an unborn infant are for its adjustment to life outside the womb, so is our faith Here and Now for our adjustment to life There and Then. Before birth those small lungs seem useless; they have no function for the embryo. But at the moment of birth they suddenly, and often vociferously, come into their destiny. In like manner, I think faith, sometimes so weak as to seem useless, will at death be the "lungs" through which adjustment to the new environment is made — lungs of the spirit through which we shall breathe the air that brings life in all its fullness, pressed down and running over.

The second help comes from the Bible. The following verses from the Old Testament are long-time friends for many of us older folk:

> ... even to your old age I am He,
>   and to gray hairs I will carry you.
> I have made, and I will bear;
>   I will carry and will save (Isaiah 46:4).

> And there shall be continuous day (it is known to the Lord), not day and not night, for at evening time there shall be light (Zechariah 14:7).

Of this last passage, Henry Durbanville writes:

> It would be no surprise that light should come at noonday; but if, when the daisies have closed their eyes, and the little birds have gone to their nests; if, when the twilight deepens, and a deep hush has come

over all Nature, a sudden burst of noonday splendour were to spread around — that would be a surprise.[5]

But that is exactly what the Oracle in Zechariah tells us — light at eventide. And in that light I truly believe we shall clearly see what God has prepared for those who love Him, which here on earth no eye has seen nor ear heard (1 Corinthians 2:9).

The third help is also from the Bible — the simple, profound words of Jesus:

> Let not your hearts be troubled; believe in God, believe also in me. In my Father's house are many rooms; if it were not so, would I have told you that I go to prepare a place for you? And when I go and prepare a place for you, I will come again and will take you to myself, that where I am you may be also (John 14:1-3).

How many times these words have brought comfort and strength to us when a loved one has died! What comfort and strength they hold for us when *our* death is near! Were all other supports gone, these words alone could give us our Fifth Blessing.

So now we are at the end of this chapter and the end of the book. Before you close it, let me say to you what our Chinese friends called to us in parting, "*Wu fu! Wu fu!*" And in warm Christian fellowship let me tell you — one and all — that I trust it will be a long time yet before you reach for your slippers.

---

[5] *The Best Is Yet to Be,* R. McCall Barbour, Edinburgh, 1957, p. 55.

APPENDIX

APPENDIX

Books of Interest for You and Me

ARTHUR, JULIETTA K., *You and Yours: How to Help Older People*, Keystone Books, 1960.

The dedication of Julietta Arthur's *You and Yours*, "To my Mother and those many other older People who want understanding, not sympathy," sets the tone of the book. Here is no "talking down" to the elderly but a "talking for" them. It is a book for the elderly and for those who are close to them.

Among the chapters are:
"Getting Along With Older People"
"Getting On in Years — Safely"
"To Work or Not to Work"
"Active Leisure, New Way for Old"

One section headed "Where to Turn for Help" gives useful information for special problems, listing the names of organizations and pamphlets, free or inexpensive.

BOUCHERON, PIERRE, *How to Enjoy Life After Sixty: A Guide to Understanding and Enjoying the Later Years*, Archer House, Inc., 1959.

This book has the flavor of a textbook, with information on health, nutrition, the importance of grooming, how to make and keep friends, and other aspects essential to the understanding and enjoyment of later years. Likening the "shock of retirement" for a person who has made no preparation for it to crashing into a stone wall, the writer offers five suggestions in preparing for retirement:

1. Reconcile yourself to the inevitable.
2. Retire *to* something not *from* something.
3. Work out carefully your money needs from all available sources. If insufficient, plan now to convert one of your hobbies into a gainful occupation.
4. Where available, seek pre-retirement counseling from the specialists.
5. Make a will and have it witnessed properly.

His chapter on hobbies includes information on the hobbies of famous men. "Retirement," says Mr. Boucheron, "is a full-time occupation. It is Big Business to you personally."

Cabot, Natalie Harris, *You Can't Count on Dying,* Houghton Mifflin Co., 1961.

This book is a library of case studies of older people who belie the customary, preconceived notions about the aged. Under the light of scientific research, one by one these notions melt away. In initiating the research, the staff at the Age Center in New England hoped through detailed documentation of the experience of aging, as revealed in the intense research with the help of one thousand patients, divided into smaller groups for successive experiments, that readers of the book would see older citizens as "people not very different" from the younger researchers themselves "except for the stress of being old and denied the privileges of social usefulness which is an inherent part of life." Readers, I believe, will agree that this hope is realized.

The staff at the Center called the older people they were studying "immigrants who have crossed a great span of time rather than space to arrive on the shore of today, the present." Older folk will find some of the comments of the researchers amusing or irritating, depending upon one's own nature. Example:

> One staff member who had been working with children said to another staff member: "I really expected the members to be more like children. After all, most of them are pretty old and it's a well-known fact that people become childlike in late age. But the members I've seen are as independent as if they were in the prime of life. It's been rather a shock."
>
> The other member of the staff: "Primarily the members are people. Each one I've interviewed has been different from the last, and it would be hard for me to classify them as exceptionally young or as about what you would expect. It seems to me that some of your own prejudices are showing."

Notable quote:

> Practice in stress gives older people a distinct advantage over their juniors. . . . As a result, they are as strong as the Rock of Gibraltar, and if a new catastrophe were to come along, they can draw abundantly on their inner resources to meet it.

COLLINS, THOMAS, *Complete Guide to Retirement,* Prentice-Hall, 1970.

The announcement on the cover of this book gives a preview of the contents inside: "In this easy-to-understand guide to retirement, Thomas Collins, well-known author of 'The Golden Years' column, discusses:

> Preparation for Retirement
> Handling Your Finances

Choosing a Place to Live
Your Retirement Residence
Making Your Wife Happy in Retirement
Making Your Husband Happy in Retirement
Your Health in Retirement
Using Your Leisure
Ways to Increase Your Income
The Woman or Man Who Retires Alone
Conquering Your Worries About Retirement"

In addition to the popularity gained through this book, Mr. Collins continues to keep in close touch with his reading public through his syndicated articles "The Golden Years" and "The Senior Forum."

CROWE, CHARLES M., *Getting Ready for Tomorrow*, Abingdon, 1959.

Although this is primarily a book for those in middle life, providing "guidance for building a happy and confident later life," it also speaks to all adults. If one has lived to threescore and five, chances are that there are still good years ahead. While "sixty-five" is "later life" for the forty-five-year-old, "eighty-five" is "later life" for the sixty-five-year-old, so even at sixty-five one can be getting ready for tomorrow.

Both the forty-five's and sixty-five's can profit from the sound advice found in the fourteen chapters.

Get Ready for Tomorrow
Grow Up as You Grow Older
Remember to Forget to Be Happy
Learn to Loaf
Cultivate a Sense of Gratitude
Keep Your Mind Active
Have Faith in Yourself
Have Fun Doing Nothing
Act Your Age
Accept Your Alternatives

Mind Your Own Business
Be Kind to Your Heart
Maintain the Forward Look
Write Your Own Obituary

Notable quote:

> If we keep a mind open to beauty and goodness, a conscience free of regret, a sense of humor that keeps us from going sour, and an attitude that shuns anger, hate, and jealousy, we will find an inner peace that passes all understanding. . . . It is then that we can enjoy what we have without envying others the enjoyment of what we don't have. Then, too, we can override our loss of status or goods, for we will know that the enjoyment of life does not depend on our circumstances nearly as much as on our spirit.

GERTMAN, SAMUEL, M.D. and ALPERT, HELEN, *Wake Up Younger!: How to Make the Most of Your Later Years*, Citadel Press, 1961.

If we have ever thought that aging is a disease, this book will convince us that we are wrong; it maintains that aging is a normal and natural process accompanied by changes. Among the suggestions to help us wake up younger is the recommendation that we hold to a feeling of self-worth—feeling good about ourselves no matter what we have or what we do not have. This self-worth depends upon our having love for others and receiving love from others, being productive, being active, being independent — and, paradoxically, being able to accept help. For many of us, this last action is the hardest of all; we don't want to be a burden. Yet gerontology has found that total independence does not and cannot exist. All our life-strands are interwoven with others. Wherever we are and wherever we go, we all need each other.

The personal glimpses into the lives of Dr. Gertman's patients liven this book and make it pleasant reading.

GROENE, THEODOR, *How to Enjoy Retirement for the Rest of Your Life,* Exposition Pres, 1957.

Beginning with a narration of a trip to South America taken with his wife after his retirement, Mr. Groene writes about hobbies, geriatric problems, advantages of maturity, food, shelter, companionship, and other aspects of retirement. His chapters "Retirement Is a Career" and "Religion for the Aging" are stimulating.

In the former chapter he recalls the classic story of the soul of a retiree who found himself in a vast expanse where he was very comfortable but lonely. Nobody came to him but one attendant who in successive periods of time brought him first whatever he wished to eat, then whatever he wished in the way of games and recreation. But when, utterly bored, the deceased retiree asked for something to do, the attendant answered, "This is one thing we cannot provide here."

Whereupon the dead retiree said, "I can't stand this place any longer. If I can't have something to do, I'd rather be in Hades."

"Well," said the attendant, "where do you think you are?"

In his chapter on religion, the author shares some of his beliefs:

> I believe that this life is only the prelude to a higher spiritual existence, the precise nature and place of which only our Master knows.
> I firmly believe in the efficacy of prayer. Not the fear-induced kind, resorted to only in time of mortal

peril, but the daily practice of giving thanks for the blessings we enjoy and asking God's help for all who are struggling under heavy burdens. Even if our fervent prayers are not answered directly in a way we can understand, the very act of praying increases our moral stamina and brings reassurance and new faith. Alexis Carrel once wrote, "As a physician, I have seen men, after all other therapy had failed, lifted out of disease and melancholy by the sincere effort of prayer."

I think of God as an all-pervading, ever-present Spirit and believe His presence is daily revealed to us in many different ways if we have the eyes to see and the mind to grasp. A sunrise, a full-blown rose, a new-born child, a purely unselfish act, the flight of a dove or a glittering, starlit sky are, to me, evidences of God's presence. Another way in which, I am sure, God makes Himself known to us is the voice of conscience which stands ceaseless guard over all our actions.

HAMILTON, (Mrs. Clarence H.) LULU SNYDER, *Your Rewarding Years*, Bobbs-Merrill Co., Inc., 1955.

"In this book, addressed to women past sixty, the author does not treat the problems of aging, but stresses the rewards." The pages are filled with stories of retirees who, although not making the headlines that Grandma Moses made, nevertheless, are great inspirations.

There's the story of Esther who, after becoming a widow, opened her home to many different groups — the Drama Reading Club, the P.T.A., Mother Singers, and others. Meeting in a home, she thought, was so much more pleasant than meeting elsewhere. In a way hers was a revival of a kind of *salon* which the French women of the eighteenth century conducted.

Another story is of Reba whose husband was killed in an accident. For three weeks after his death she was able to carry out plans made earlier for a reception for visiting musicians from Europe. "Then suddenly" — Reba's own words — "I realized all was gone, not only my husband who had been the center of all my living, but my home, my source of income, my status too. Everything I had been doing for twenty-five years was no longer mine to do."

Those of us who have gone through a similar experience know what she means. We may say, "The bottom dropped out," but, like Reba, we have to come back to the growing edge of life. She found that edge when, after a year wholly outside the academic community, she reentered the social environment with which she was familiar, became director of a new house for graduate students and unmarried faculty, and found her spirit healed.

Stories like these make Mrs. Hamilton's book one of fellowship and inspiration for other "Esther's" and "Reba's." Her chapter on death, the last in the book, has been referred to above in the last chapter of this book.

HERSEY, JEAN and ROBERT, *These Rich Years: A Journal of Retirement*, Scribner, 1969.

An ex-advertising man and his wife tell how, during their first three years of retirement, they made the transition from one way of living to another, each way involving meaningful and rewarding activities. They take the reader into all aspects of their living, making their book, a subjective approach to the so-called years of leisure, optimistic and refreshing.

The *Library Journal* refers to this book as "a can't-put-it-down story of human interest. One of the best, most helpful books on retirement of recent years."

KLEEMEIER, ROBERT W., ed., *Aging and Leisure*, Oxford University Press, 1961.

Nineteen writers contributed articles to produce this book described as a "research perspective into the meaningful use of time." Among the articles are the following:

>Time, Activity, and Leisure (How people use their time).
>Work and Patterns of Retirement (Work in the lives of older people).
>Cultural Differences in the Life Cycle and Concept of Time (How St. Lawrence Eskimos, Japanese, Burmese, and Indians use their leisure time).
>Meaningful Living in Mature Years.

The writers found that decline in morale was strongly related to exclusion from activities which provide achievement, status, and recognition. The main contention is that "not any activity, but only activities that provide status, achievement, and recognition can lift morale, and that those that are not basically satisfying needs do not contribute much to the individual's adjustment."

KUTNER, BERNARD and others, *Five Hundred Over Sixty*, A Community Survey on Aging, Russell Sage Foundation, 1956.

This book is a comprehensive report of a study made at the Adult Counseling Center in the Kips Bay-Yorkville Health Center, New York City, of five hundred noninstitutionalized persons over the age of sixty. Four specific problems were dealt with: (1) problems of personal adjustment, (2) factors affecting or affected by health, (3) the use of community health centers, and (4) attitudes toward health and social centers.

Much is made of morale. Case histories make interesting reading, and for the scientifically-minded among us, time spent in studying the many tables may prove more interesting than time spent doing puzzles. (The non-scientifically-minded among us may find the puzzles less puzzling.)

A valuable part of the book is the extensive bibliography (pp. 308-335) at the end. The date of the printing of this book and even a cursory examination of the titles given will show that problems of the aging were of deep concern two decades ago.

LaFarge, John, S.J., *Reflections on Growing Old,* Doubleday and Co., 1962.

A delightful, contemplative piece of writing. Referred to above (chs. 5, 8), this book bears rereading not once but several times. It is the kind of book that becomes a friend. Coming from the mind of one who belongs to the Society of Jesus (S.J.), the slim volume bears testimony to the deep religious life of the writer. In it the Reverend La Farge invites us to read and ponder upon the words of life given us in the Scriptures.

In old age "the words take on new meaning, unlock doors that heretofore were barred by confusion and misunderstanding. We begin to see what life is all about, what the Creator has made of us and what He is trying to fashion in our minds and hearts. . . .

In the later years of life you will be richly rewarded if you can afford to enjoy the time of meditation and reflection. You can let much of the world go by; you can think more often and more affectionately of the new life that is being born within you."

Would that all of us might have the same attitude toward aging that this writer has.

"I believe," says he, "old age is a gift, a very precious gift, not a calamity. Since it is a gift, I thank God for it daily."

LEGLER, HENRY, *How to Make the Rest of Your Life the Best of Your Life,* Pocket Books, 1970.

The cover advertises this book as a "practical plan for learning how *not* to retire from life when you retire from work." And on the flyleaf we read:

WHAT THIS BOOK WILL DO FOR YOU

It will:
1. Tell you how to give your life a new purpose, a new meaning, a new importance.
2. Show you how to make new friendships quickly and easily.
3. Bring you a new way to cultivate self-confidence, inner peace and spiritual strength.
4. Tell you how to overcome the worries that burden your life.
5. Give you the secret of feeling youthful indefinitely.
6. Provide you with a tested formula for marital happiness in your retirement years.
7. Give you the inspiring stories of more than one hundred everyday people who refused to grow old.
8. Tell you how to make younger people like you instantly.
9. Give you twelve reasons why the rest of your life can be the best of your life.

The book is faithful to its promise. I could not rest until I had finished the book, so lively is the writing, so full of substance are the pages.

WARE, GEORGE W., *The New Guide to Happy Retirement,* Crown, 1969.

This book deals with finances, diet, housing, places to live at home and abroad, and other subjects of interest to retirees, affluent and not so affluent. The *Journal of Home Economics,* December, 1968, praises the book as "enjoyable, lending itself to leisure reading." *Library Journal,* 15 December 1968, comments, "George Ware, a trained economist . . . has compiled a down-to-earth, practical handbook, overwhelming in the mass of information on all branches of his subject."

WHITMAN, VIRGINIA, *Around the Corner From Sixty,* Moody Press, 1967.

This book is brimful of good advice for one "who is approaching the sixth decade or has already passed that milestone."

Be open-minded, flexible, courageous, grateful, helpful, hospitable — these are among the virtues which produce a meaningful "old age." Part 1 ends with chapters entitled "Have a Goal and Hang Onto It" and "Take Hold and Take Heart." Pleasant reading, with an abundance of examples of men and women who have made retirement years satisfying years.

Part 2 is inspirational. With Christ as our transformer and the Bible as our handbook, Mrs. Whitman shows how the spirit will be equipped and "ready for a rendezvous."